"John Lankford's *The Answer Is Leader[...]* [...] leadership fails for so many organizat[...] steps, and recommendations for impr[...] excellent leadership. Executives will [...] enhance organizational culture, improve leadership, and g[...]

—**Joseph M. Tasse, FACHE, executive-in-residence, Sloan Program in Health Administration, Cornell University (past president of several acute care hospitals)**

"Leaders create the culture and the culture creates the results in any organization. John Lankford's new book is a step-by-step guide on how to create a winning culture from someone who walks his talk."

—**Orrin Woodward, *Inc. Magazine* Top 20 Leader, *New York Times* best-selling author**

"There is no question that quality and trust are the key elements to an effective leadership team. John really 'nails it' on the measurement, accountability, and culture model of an exceptional company. As a result of implementing these principles, performing an assessment, and creating alignment, we have grown our company 23 percent this past year. John has been an invaluable asset to our leadership development program."

—**Jeffrey L. Brittan, CEO, StructureTec Group**

"John Lankford's career has focused on improving the quality of executive leadership and enhancing corporate culture. He now has put together the tools that made him so successful in his book *The Answer Is Leadership*. His 'winning formula' emphasizes an environment that values appreciation, vulnerability, and accountability. It is a clear guide for any executive who has a passion for improvement."

—**Dick Beadle, founder, Vistage Michigan**

"I've watched John coach C-level leaders for several years and have seen the excellent results of his efforts. This book distills his years of accumulated knowledge and will be a great tool for leaders at all levels."

—**Michael Weeks, PhD, Baptist University, director of strategy and leadership**

"Leadership guru, John Lankford takes readers on a deep dive into the ingredients that make a great leader, and the pitfalls to avoid along the way. With over 30 years of experience, John offers sage advice on the secrets of successful strategic planning and team building. His unique insights into the essential components for cultural change, coupled with a robust accountability system, will revolutionize your company. *The Answer Is Leadership* is a must-have tool for leaders of today, and a valuable tutorial for leaders of tomorrow."

—Dick Rolfe, CEO, The Dove Foundation

"*The Answer Is Leadership* promises a blueprint for leadership and delivers marvelously. John Lankford gives you the guidance every CEO needs about culture, planning and executing strategy, and developing top talent in practical, effective ways. It is well-researched and backed up by John's extensive experience helping business owners and leadership teams improve results. I especially appreciate the examples that John provides so that you can benchmark your own organization against the best of the best. While novels are often called 'epic' when they are sweeping in scope, I would apply the same description to *The Answer Is Leadership.* It provides the depth and breadth that you will want to keep among your top leadership resources."

—Andrew Neitlich, founder and director, Center for Executive Coaching

"Identifying and growing the talent of leaders in your organization is critical to creating a successful company that stands out from the crowd. The tools and systems explained by John in his book are the perfect guide to help companies be more profitable and successful."

—Mike Semanco, president and COO, Hitachi Business Finance

"*The Answer is Leadership ... What Is the Question?* addresses the most important and often overlooked components of leadership: providing tangible and quantifiable tools that create the self-awareness of an individual leader's strengths and how those strengths impact others. This book defines the role of an organizational leader who drives the value of culture. For those individuals and organizations who seek to reach the summit, *The Answer is Leadership ... What Is the Question?* is the pathway to SUCCESS."

—Michael Pacholek, president, Summit Assessment Solutions

"John has created a superb, practical, insightful, easy to read set of skills, best practices, and tools for today's senior leader. This book is a must read for any manager with a desire to turbocharge their leadership skills to achieve tangibly improved results."

—Brian Lee, CSP, CEO and founder, Custom Learning Systems Group Ltd., HealthCare Service Excellence Institute

THE ANSWER IS LEADERSHIP

What Is the Question?

**How the best CEOs
build high-performing
companies**

THE ANSWER IS
LEADERSHIP

What Is the Question?

**How the best CEOs
build high-performing
companies**

John Lankford

Published by Premier Executive Forums
48268 Hilltop Drive E.
Plymouth, Michigan 48170
www.PremierExecutiveForums.com

Printed in the United States of America
First Printing

Publisher's Cataloging-in-Publication

Lankford, John, 1950-
    The answer is leadership : what is the question? : how the best CEOs build high-
performing companies / John Lankford.

        pages : illustrations, charts ; cm

    Includes bibliographical references and index.
    ISBN 978-0-9963216-0-0 (softcover)
    ISBN 978-0-9963216-2-4 (Mobipocket)
    ISBN 978-0-9963216-1-7 (EPUB)

    1. Leadership. 2. Performance--Management. 3. Organizational effectiveness.
    4. Corporate culture. 5. Customer services. 6. Executive ability. 7. Success in
business. I. Title.

HD57.7 .L36 2015
658.4/092

This book is dedicated to my WHY (Why do I do what I do?), my wife Karen and my daughter Logan. My why has two components. The first is to secure my family's financial future. The second is more closely tied to my mission: as I help business owners grow their businesses, I help secure jobs for American families. Entrepreneurs/small businesses employ 120 million people every day. I want to positively impact or help create new jobs and the cultures where people go to work every day, and bring one million new jobs to America. So this book is dedicated to my family and putting Americans back to work.

This book is dedicated to the hundreds of thousands of entrepreneurs who are willing to take all the risks that come with being an entrepreneur. Business owners have none of the certainty of being an employee in someone else's company.

This book is also is dedicated to those small-minded leaders who would not give me a chance because my undergraduate and master's degrees in business were not from big, prestigious schools. Yet it is also dedicated to Sheila Johnson, who asked me to become the CEO of the Innisbrook Leadership Institute.

The contents of this book would not be possible if it were not for the learnings I had from my father and mother. Both of my parents were raised in the South, so I was raised with those Southern values. My dad, who never went to college, gave back to his community so often over 30 years that today there is a city park named after him. And in 2010, I was recognized as the Abundance Coach of the Year for giving and helping those in need—thanks Dad!

Finally, this book is dedicated to Dale Sawickie, my high school football coach. Why Dale? One day at a practice session, Dale saw me standing upright at the end of a play. As a defensive end, he expected me to always be active and moving. Still today I can hear him yelling at me: "Damn it, John, hit someone, even if it's the wrong team." I'm not sure why that comment stuck with me, but ever since then I have become obsessed with delivering results—hit someone!

Contents

Acknowledgments

I first must thank my wife Karen, who has been a nurse for 31 years, and my daughter Logan, who just graduated business school and Michigan State University (with a very high grade point average, and who accepted an offer at Toyota six months before graduating). Both have sacrificed and significantly contributed their support and encouragement to the stories in this 30-year journey of book contents, including some restarts as I switched companies.

I would like to thank Mike Flaherty, who started his career at Ford Motor Company as a janitor and retired as a member of its management team. He taught me many lessons about leadership. Two that stuck with me were to always deliver results to your manager faster than they ask and never, never let your manager be surprised or blindsided. Mike was a great mentor and very focused on delivering results.

Some other people I would like to thank are Mike Pacholek, Jennifer Hines, Heather Christie, and Vince Lee. Vince may be the most passionate leader I have ever met when it comes to working with people and developing a great culture. I would like to thank Andrew Neitlich and Corey Crowder, who helped me in many ways, including contributing to my first book about career transitions. And I would like to thank Brad Sugars for creating the world's largest business coaching franchise and the model that trained and certified me to coach business owners of all sizes.

Thanks go to all the leaders who have taken the time to write their stories in books that I have read and learned from—I love to read.

I would like to recognize Eric Hohauser and Lori Williams. They are clearly two of the greatest connectors I have met in the last 20 years. They each could write a book on developing relationships and giving to others.

I would like to recognize the best role model of a Christian leader I have ever met on this planet, Jeffrey L. Brittan. Jeff founded Christian Business Round Table meetings to talk about business issues and invite people to learn more about Christianity. He is such a great mentor.

I would like to thank Nancy Badore, who selected me to be part of the executive team to develop the top 2,000 leaders at Ford Motor Company for many years. I learned so much that eventually contributed to my ability to be an executive coach.

Finally, I would like to recognize the hundreds of business owners who have allowed me to coach them to grow their company; I have learned something from every one of them and still continue to do so.

Foreword

For more than two decades now, I've been advising senior executives in organizations of all shapes and sizes on how to grow and develop leaders in order to fully leverage talent in pursuit of their business objectives. Here is a piece of advice for anyone in a position of leadership at any level: Pay attention to John Lankford and the important lessons he is teaching in this book, *The Answer Is Leadership*.

Why? The reason is that leadership really matters, and this book offers a systematic approach to understanding the current state of leadership in your organization, where you need to be, and how to bridge the gap.

I love this book because, like my own work, it is does not pretend there are short-cuts to creating a culture of strong, effective leadership. There are no short-cuts in here, but rather a comprehensive, step-by-step process for conducting your own needs assessment/gap analysis for determining your leadership development priorities, making an actionable plan, doing the hard work of identifying and developing leadership talent, and maintaining the kind of ongoing due-diligence that ensures—and magnifies—the ongoing return on investment that comes from implementing leadership development very, very well. This is a platinum approach to leadership development. So if you are looking for the cheap, easy version, you might as well just stop reading now. But if you want to learn how to do it right—and from a very wise pro—then keep going!

Leadership in today's world involves a lot of complexities. Consider the following:

☐ **People come and go**

That's always been true. But employment relationships today in the modern economy are far more short term and fluid than they have been before. So you are always losing good people. And you are always trying to get new people on board and up to speed. On top of that, one great employee is worth more than three or four or five mediocre employees. Sometimes you have to go to great lengths to effectively reward, retain, and develop the very best employees.

☐ **Constant change comes at you from every direction**

Technology, the markets, the weather, geopolitics, micropolitics, customer requirements, vendor requirements, employee requirements—change regularly forces rework. Getting change right makes that rework manageable.

☐ **There is interdependency**

More and more of our work involves lots of moving parts and, therefore, lots of counterparts here, there, and everywhere. Most people must rely on many others inside and outside their immediate work group in order to do their own work.

☐ **Resources are constrained**

Everybody is expected nowadays to do more with less. Increasingly, people report that they are making do with tighter and tighter resources, and longer and more complex supply lines, with shorter and shorter lead times. Often people find themselves trying to do their jobs with what they feel are insufficient resources.

☐ **Employees are human**

Human beings have weaknesses as well as strengths. Humans are not always great at self-management. They have habits, and not always good ones. Not only that, but everybody has bad days. Some people have bad weeks, months, even years. Productivity and quality of work are highly variable, sometimes due to employee performance. On top of all that, humans have attitudes, and not always good ones.

This book will help you look at your organization's culture and the role of leaders in a whole new way as you anticipate, plan for, and navigate through all of these complexities. You won't find lots of fancy, new ideas in this book. But fancy, new ideas are so often "flavors of the month" and NOT what you should be looking for in a book about leadership!

I promise you, what's missing in the leadership culture of most organizations is NOT another "flavor of the month," but rather a systematic approach and a comprehensive, step-by-step process. That's what this book offers.

Our own research shows clearly that when organizations ignore the rigors of a systematic approach, the consequences are significant and costly:

1. You will be more likely to make suboptimal hiring decisions.
2. New hires will be more likely to get on board and up to speed more slowly.
3. Employees will have lower productivity and make more mistakes.
4. Employees will be more likely to have negative attitudes, as well as more conflicts with each other.
5. Employees will be less likely to learn new, technical skills and also less likely to improve their nontechnical skills.
6. High performers will be more likely to leave.
7. Your culture will produce declining revenues and profits.
8. Customers will not return as often.

On the other hand, when organizations practice the fundamentals of comprehensive leadership development with rigor and consistency, as John Lankford lays them out, everything goes much better:

1. You will hire better people.
2. They will get on board and up to speed more quickly and effectively.
3. Employees will do more work better and faster.
4. Employees will have higher morale, and therefore, manifest much better attitudes.
5. Employees will be more likely to learn and grow their technical skills, as well as their soft skills, on an ongoing basis.
6. You will be much better able to push out the low performers and retain the high performers.
7. With strong leadership, your organization will experience increased revenues and profits.
8. Customers will become raving fans.

This book is a rock-solid guide to remaking your approach to leadership development. Read it, reread it, and then take action!

—Bruce Tulgan, founder of RainmakerThinking, Inc.® and the author of numerous books, including *It's Okay to Be the Boss* (2007), *The 27 Challenges Managers Face* (2014), and *Not Everyone Gets a Trophy* (revised and updated 2016)

Preface

American businesses are a mess. Not all American businesses, but too many of them. Did I get your attention? Good, that's what I was aiming for.

For the most part, American privately held companies are doing a very poor job of serving their customers. And the owners, and often founders of those companies, wonder why their businesses aren't more profitable or more productive, or why they have high employee turnover.

Yet there are exceptions. There are some companies out there doing it right. By that I mean they have reached the top of their industry and they know how to maintain their position. Not by chance or luck, but by strategically creating the right kind of company culture. Doing so leads to happy employees, who in turn treat customers very well. And that all has to do with the company's leaders—having the right people in the right positions and making leadership development, on all levels, a business priority.

So many business owners and/or executives don't really understand the business implications of how being complacent with who's on their management team and how well trained and developed they are is undermining their business. It's almost not being talked about. Well, I want to challenge the way business owners and/or executives think about running companies.

For privately held business owners, my experience is that most of them have learned how to be very effective in running certain parts of their business. Unfortunately, it's rare that I speak with a CEO or an executive and find them to be highly competent at "developing talent." There are many reasons for this gap. One reason is that most business schools and the top executive education institutions in the world focus on other more sexy leadership talents and skills. Yet the level I'm describing is for a CEO to be so skilled at "developing talent" that he or she could stand in front of an audience of managers and teach a class on the subject. Can you?

I hope reading this book will inspire you to make a new decision to take the subject of "developing talent" more seriously, starting with your entire management team. This book is written for people in decision-making authority positions. They're the ones who created the mess, and they're the only ones who can change it.

How can I be so bold as to make that statement? Because of my background and experience.

I've been a frontline supervisor in a plant at Ford Motor Company (a foreman on an assembly line), the CEO of a company, and at most levels in between. So I've been at every leadership level in a business. I was part of the executive development team at Ford Motor Company for 18 years, helping develop their top 2,000 leaders around the world. I have designed and built a leadership development model for two large healthcare systems. (You'll read more about these ventures in an upcoming chapter.) I've worked and partnered with some of the most prestigious institutions to develop current and future leaders, two of them being the Center for Creative Leadership and the University of Michigan Business School.

I have also worked for the world's largest business coaching franchise for five years. In fact, I was a partner in one of the franchises. Out of the 450 offices in North America, I was the number one rated business advisor in North America four years in a row, based on my sales and client results. For more than 90 percent of those four years, I was working with privately owned businesses to design and implement change, and in every instance the competence of the management team increased.

Much of my corporate background is in the healthcare and manufacturing industries. Those industries are extraordinarily process and systems driven, and everything is about improving the process. I've taken what I've learned in corporate America and applied it to entrepreneurs. And I believe I have a unique perspective on the challenges you're facing, if you are a business owner.

I wrote this book because I wanted to share with you what those top companies—the best of the best—are doing, and show you how you can apply those same principles, processes, and systems to your own company, regardless of size. The solutions I'll be outlining in *The Answer Is Leadership ... What Is the Question?* are results-based, tested, and proven. This book is a collection of those best business practices that I've learned through my 33 years of working with executives from Fortune 100 companies to small entrepreneurs and everybody in between. Much of what I'll be presenting is based on my own experience. The rest comes from studying the experts, either reading about what they've written, hearing them speak, or working with them directly. Therefore, I'll be providing real world examples and quoting some well-recognized names, such names as Jim Collins and Keith McFarland.

And what you may find unique about my writing style is that I like to ask questions. I truly find it valuable to make you think about the subject as it relates to your company.

Throughout my years in the corporate environment, I've come to realize that there are basically three types of company leaders, as illustrated in Figure 1. There are approximately 8 percent who are exceptional, the best of the best. Then there are somewhere in the neighborhood of 22 percent who are working hard at becoming the best of the best. They're using some of the methodologies, skills, and best practices, but they're not there yet. And finally, there are the approximately 70 percent who are close-minded, do not use outside resources effectively and, on balance, continue to run their companies the same way they did three to 10 years ago. This book is written for that 22 percent who want to improve, those who are looking for solutions that work. They're open to learning faster, more effective ways

Figure 1

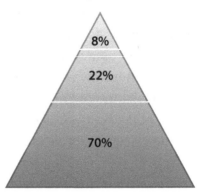

to improve their systems and the productivity of their staff.

Okay, let's cut to the chase, there are fundamentally only two reasons you, the reader, will call me after reading this book: a.) your company is currently doing well, but you're nowhere near the vision you had for what is possible, or b.) your company is stuck, has plateaued, and is honestly not performing very well financially, and you cannot seem to break through and take your company to the next level.

I want to help you clearly see the connection between the problems businesses have created and the solutions that are possible. My challenge to you, the reader, is to better understand the huge impact leaders at all levels have on your company's culture, employees, customers, profitability, and ultimately, your company's future. More importantly, there is a solution to every business problem you're currently facing. That solution, and the answer, is *leadership*. Because of how integrated many of these learnings are, you may notice some important points are repeated—by design. My idea was to give you a blueprint, a model you can follow, if you're serious about outperforming your competition. If not, this will just be a fun read.

Introduction

I speak in front of a lot of audiences, at conferences and other events. Whether their annual revenue is $5 million a year or $500 million, I've probably asked 10,000 executives—CEOs and presidents of companies—the same question: "When you go on vacation, what one or two thoughts do you continue to think about when it comes to your business?" More than 90 percent respond that they think about how they can increase revenues. That usually translates into how they can land more customers, retain the customers they have, and improve cash flow overall.

How about you? What keeps you up at night when it comes to your business? What can't you stop thinking about?

- ☐ Is your company as profitable as it could be?
- ☐ Is your business growing?
- ☐ Are your operations running smoothly and are they very efficient?
- ☐ Are you experiencing high employee turnover?
- ☐ What's your customer loyalty level like?
- ☐ How long will your business run at a high level without you?

When you look at how companies attract new business and how they retain the business they have, I am convinced that the kind of company and culture you've built, and how well your company delivers on its promise to customers every single day, is a direct reflection of the quality of your leadership. What do I mean by that? I've found that what separates companies at the top of their game from their competition comes down to one word: leadership. So I set out to prove in these pages that the quality of your leadership team—senior level leaders, middle management, and frontline supervisors—will be directly reflected in the kind of culture your company has, how well you attract new business, and how well you retain customers.

How am I going to do that? How am I going to prove to you that how your company is operating today—good or bad, profitable or unprofitable—is based on your company's leaders? I'm going to take you on a benchmarking trip covering my 30-plus years inside of companies big and small, benchmarking people who are the best. Through my experiences and examples of my work, I'm going to show you just how the "best of the best" have been and are maintaining their positions at the top of their industries.

Most organizations, most leaders, don't understand how to identify one of their current processes or systems and then go study somebody who's the best at it. When you go benchmarking, you gather information, study it, adapt it, and then take action on it. If you want to improve your processes, your company's talent, and the quality of your leadership, why wouldn't you benchmark what other people are doing and learn from them?

For example, I was part of a task force building the most high-tech cement plant in North America. We went on a benchmarking trip to study a French fry factory, where trains of potatoes went in one side and departed out the other side of the plant in 18-wheeler trucks delivering the ready-to-cook fries to Burger King and McDonald's. The two industries have nothing in common, yet we were there to study processes, because this factory was known for its process efficiencies.

I was also working for a major automaker when we were hosting more than 60 benchmarking trips a year made by companies you may have heard of—Harley Davidson, Toyota, and other big names. They all wanted to see what we were doing, what made us so different. I was this automaker's team consultant for three years.

I believe that no matter which issue we're talking about, whether it's market share, cash flow, revenue, finding good people, having turnover, or competitors taking customers away, the answer is the same. Those results are happening because of the way your leadership team is running your company. It always comes back to leadership; leadership is the problem and leadership is the solution.

I have observed and learned that there are a small percentage of business leaders who are exceptional, running companies that last and grow over time. These are companies that consistently outperform their competition in their marketplace. In the chapters that follow, I'll describe my formula, my blueprint for strategies that work. I have seen these strategies work time and time again, and not just a little, but at the level of helping a Big Three automaker build the best engine plant in the world. Those strategies have also taken a major healthcare system from having high turnover to saving millions of dollars, while delivering higher-quality care and becoming recognized as one of the best places to work.

Here are some of the topics we'll cover in upcoming chapters:

- ☐ Effective benchmarking
- ☐ The behaviors great leaders demonstrate
- ☐ Leadership "truths" related to your business
- ☐ The skills required to be a top-notch leader
- ☐ The importance of alignment in your organization
- ☐ Getting customers to rave about your company
- ☐ Why employee accountability is essential
- ☐ Assessing your leadership team
- ☐ Measuring the effectiveness of your culture
- ☐ Providing leaders with feedback
- ☐ Building individual development plans
- ☐ The nine core talent management systems
- ☐ Developing your current leaders
- ☐ Tracking your management training and development

☐ Using executive coaching to execute on a higher level

☐ Overcoming resistance when you start making culture changes

All of these factors influence your company's culture. And that culture affects your employees' experiences and your customers' experiences. For those of you who are not sure what the word "culture" means, culture is the way you do things in your company and the work environment you create.

There's a lot of research out there to support the belief that when you build a high-performing culture, you must start by ensuring your current management team is fit to execute. Do you currently have strong leaders in every management position in your company? Do you have a culture that attracts top talent and new customers? Given all the change that's occurring—the availability of cash, customer demands, government regulations, your competition, products and services, and technology—you need to have a strategic plan to develop your management team. What if your current culture was producing an extraordinary customer experience, reflected by how your employees treat customers? How would that affect your market share and your cash flow?

How many companies can you name that deliver an extraordinary customer experience every time? I know your answer is a very short list. If a company delivers extraordinary service, that reputation will become a true marketing strategy. In today's marketplace, a business that provides an extraordinary customer experience will steal market share and customers from its competition.

I would like leaders to have an increased appreciation for how much they impact the design and functionality of the culture of their company, and what that means to the bottom line and future of their business. Most company owners do not really understand what it's costing them by not having a strategic plan to develop their current and future leadership team. They're doing other things to try and be more profitable and improve cash flow, but they're not dealing with the root cause of the problem, which is that their management at all three levels (senior leaders/executives, middle management, and frontline managers/supervisors) is just not fit to execute. So they're not prepared to manage and lead an industry leading organization.

The quality of your leadership team will be reflected in your Profit and Loss statements, your operations, your cash flow, by how you attract top talent, and by the turnover in your company. In great, top-performing companies, there's a commitment to process improvement and building a great place to work. There's a commitment to identifying and developing great talent. And I'll prove it.

It's a leader's responsibility to understand how to design a high-performing culture. And it's been my experience that most organizations do not achieve their potential because they do not have the right leaders in the right positions. When I say leadership, I'm talking about leaders on those three fundamental levels, including frontline managers who are often left out of formal development activities. Building sustainably profitable companies starts with a high-performing leadership team on all three levels.

Does your strategic plan, regardless of the size of your company, include talent? Does your budget reflect that plan or that section of your business plan? Everybody tells me, "People are our greatest asset," and I say, "Show me your budget for developing talent." Ninety-eight percent of the time, their budget does not reflect that talent is their greatest asset, they don't devote the money or time to developing their workforce, and they wonder why executive search firms hire their most valuable players away. Too many executives are giving lip service to the subject of the quality of their leadership team. And they don't know how to change from the way they're operating now to how they should be operating, in ways that will make a difference. What about training your frontline associates, because the best of the best companies do? The American Society for Training and Development, studying best practices around the country, recently found that average companies spend about $1,000 per employee per year to develop their frontline associates and about 30.5 hours of training per employee.

Every single topic or business issue related to your company is the result of a business decision or lack of a decision. It starts at the top, but most CEOs do not have an effective talent management strategy and have not created a winning culture. It doesn't matter what the business does. Rarely do customers leave impressed beyond their expectations. There just aren't many businesses that provide that kind of customer experience. And it all starts with leadership.

There are approximately 44 million tax returns filed by businesses small to large in America every year. They employ millions of people. According to Eric Hohauser, vice president of executive search firm Harvey Hohauser & Associates, "private businesses in America supply 69 percent of the federal government's tax revenues." A few thousand of them close their doors every day. And there are dozens of mergers and acquisitions that take place every month. Those actions all cost people jobs. Over the last two decades, too many jobs have left America because they can be done better, faster, and cheaper in other places, and some of that work could be brought back home, but not if the companies can't be as profitable here in America. When we can start focusing on leadership and creating the kind of business structures that build financially stable businesses delivering high-quality products and services at an affordable price, then we'll begin to bring business back to America, and there will be fewer businesses going under, and that is my mission.

So, are you looking for a new methodology, a new formula, a new blueprint to change the future of your business? Do you want to change your story, or are you going to continue to tolerate the way your current leadership team is performing? If you're a CEO or president of a company and are reading this book, you ought to recognize that you really have only four choices when it comes to the people and talent in your company:

1. You can continue to tolerate the way your management team is running your business today,
2. You can selectively go out and buy new talent with an executive search firm,

3. You can develop the talent you have,
   and/or
4. You can do some combination of numbers two and three.

How does all this impact businesses right now? Why should you have a system in place to assess and develop current people in leadership positions on all three levels? A company, private or public, will never outperform its leadership team. Ever. Why? You cannot expect an organization to execute its plan without having the right leaders in place.

And what about your future leaders? Do you have a process in place to assess and develop leaders on an ongoing basis? What will your business look like three to five years from now? The game changing decision is to also invest in the development of your future leadership team. Most leaders don't really understand how to develop talent, and have done a poor job at developing people that are already in leadership positions. If you're not even developing the leaders you have, when are you going to put a system in place to be able to identify and develop the next generation of leaders? It's not just about developing current leaders, it's about developing future leaders, too. In fact, your business depends on it.

Your experiences may be similar to my stories, or they may be different, but I'm positive that after reading this book you should feel the compelling need to ensure your entire management team has mastered the fundamentals of leadership.

CHAPTER 1

What's the Current State of America's Business?

Many CEOs assume that others share their understanding of corporate goals. "When challenged to list the company's 10 highest priorities, five top execs listed 23 and only two appeared on more than one list."

—Ericka Herb, Keith Leslie, and Colin Price, "Teamwork at the Top," *McKinsey Quarterly*

Recently, I asked an audience how they would rate service in America today. Would it be a "C," average, where you just get what you pay for, or is it above average? About 90 percent of the audience said the service they encountered is about a "C," or the get-what-you-pay-for kind. And it turns out most of us are surprised with "A" grade, exceptional service.

According to Bob Pritchard, quoted in a *Harvard Business Review* article, 62 percent of buyers do not buy repeatedly from the same source. Add to that a 2013 study by Edelman Trust Barometer, showing that trust in America has declined for the last five years. People do not trust CEOs and executives like they used to, nor do they trust politicians, school boards, or the media. Trust in America has simply continued to decline.

If a customer's experience of doing business with a company is less than magnificent, they go somewhere else next time, or they'll simply buy the cheapest. However, we know people will pay more for great service, and great service only comes from employees who love working for their company and put in discretionary effort every day. When your customers have that kind of experience with your employees, they come back. In fact, they tell others about you. Then your culture and customers' experiences become a marketing strategy. Those people become loyal customers. And at the end of the day, loyalty is a huge measure of success.

Yet most companies do not have a marketing or communication plan focused on the customer experience before, during, and after the purchase. Most companies spend all their marketing and communication dollars trying to land new customers. But what about a plan for retaining the customers they already serve?

I believe leaders don't really understand that building high-performing cultures produces extraordinary customer experiences. Those experiences translate into greater profits, and ultimately, sustained growth. Most executives don't understand how a strong company culture could significantly improve their margins and their profitability by changing their customers' experiences. And you can't do that unless you have a workplace everybody loves, where they get a lot done, and every day they give you that discretionary 5-10 percent effort.

What about *Your* Company?

How is your company performing? Do you have repeat customers? How satisfied are you with the current condition of your business and the direction in which it's heading?

Premier Executive Forums and Naviga Business Services conducted a survey in 2012 in which 33,000 executives were asked some key questions about their business. (Premier Executive Forums is my company and Naviga Business Services is an executive search firm that specializes in finding executives for marketing and sales positions.) The executives were asked about how satisfied they were with their company's leadership, execution, and differentiation. You can see the results in Figure 2 on the next page.

More than a third of those asked said their company is not effective at converting its strategic plan into an operational plan to ensure organizational alignment. More than a quarter said that executing the company's operational plan for the year is not a strength of its leadership team. More than a third said they would rehire less than 50 percent of their current management team. Almost 40 percent said their organization does not have a plan in place for developing leaders. And more than half said their company does not have an effective succession plan in place! Yet more than three-fourths of respondents said having a "scorecard" of the company's key performance indicators (KPI) would be valuable, they would invest the time and money in its development, and they felt they would greatly benefit from having an executive coach.

According to respondents, the relative success in differentiating their own organization from that of the competition is another area where improvement could be gained. Just more than half (56%) of respondents said they were satisfied with the ability to differentiate themselves from their competition, 44% of executives were NOT satisfied.

—Premier Executive Forums National 2012 Study

What Really Is the Problem?

So, what exactly is the problem in the American business landscape today? It all comes down to this: How leaders treat their employees is how their employees will treat their customers. If you want to get to the root cause of the problem, go all the way back upstream and ask yourself, "Do I have the kind of management team that will take this company to the next level?" The answer is rarely yes, because over time, leaders have come to tolerate leading an average company. The disconnect is that they say they want to grow the business, but their actions toward the strategic development of their entire leadership team

Figure 2

National Study of Executives in More Than 33,000 Companies *Conducted by Premier Executive Forums and Naviga Business Services*	
39.6% disagreed	Do you have a system in place for developing leaders within your organization?
34.4% said less than 50%	What percentage of your entire management team can articulate their individual top four measurable priorities?
39.6% said less than 50%	What percentage of your organization executes its plan of top priorities consistently?
36.1% said less than 50%	What percentage of your entire management team would you rehire as top performers?
53.5% disagreed	My organization has an effective succession plan in place.
36.6% dissatisfied or extremely dissatisfied	How satisfied are you overall with your company's use of your annual performance appraisal process (accountability) for your sales team?
88.8% agreed or strongly agreed	It would be valuable to have a one-page scorecard of my company's "key performance indicators" to provide a weekly/monthly pulse of how the company is performing.
75.9% agreed or strongly agreed	I would invest time and money to develop a scorecard of my company's "key performance indicators" to provide a weekly/monthly pulse of how the company is performing.
26.7% disagreed	My company does an effective job of strategic planning.
34.4% disagreed	My company effectively converts our strategic plan into an operational plan to ensure organizational alignment.
26.4% disagreed	Executing your operational plan for the year is a strength of your leadership team.
81.6% agreed	Members of my management team would benefit greatly by having an executive coach to confide in and help define our development.

would say they prefer to "tolerate" current performance. They won't say that, but that's exactly what they do. That's what their budget and their actions suggest. While many business owners understand the word "culture," they don't do much to actively build a customer attracting culture.

Most CEOs and most management teams do a relatively poor job of dealing with people who have bad attitudes or do not demonstrate the company values, or those who are poor, "D," performers. Leaders in almost every organization I encounter can name the "D" performers. Their coworkers actually like it when "D" performers call in sick, for many reasons, including that best performers do not like working with "D" performers.

You can take a walk in any company and stop 10 employees and ask them: "If you had a magic wand and could get rid of two coworkers, who would they be?" Most of them will say the same two names. Everybody knows who they are, but management won't do anything about it. So often these leaders have not been trained or are not skilled in helping people improve their performance, or coaching these mediocre employees out of the organization. Sometimes leaders do have these skills, but they don't have the courage to use them and are not held accountable to do so.

A weak management team directly affects company sustainability. To me, sustainability indicates a company is consistently growing. It can be controlled growth, but it's growth nonetheless. While average companies typically do not have long-term, sustainable profitability, there are exceptions. Yet a seven-year chart of their profitability will look like an EKG chart (it's up, it's down, it's up). Some people get lucky, meaning the right place, right time kind of thing. But most CEOs cannot count on long-term, sustainable profit growth year after year, if 25 to 50 percent of their management team members are "C" performers.

I've already mentioned "A," "B," "C," and "D" performers. Throughout this book, I'll reference and talk about levels of performance. Figure 3 shows a simple scale we use when adding an accountability

Figure 3

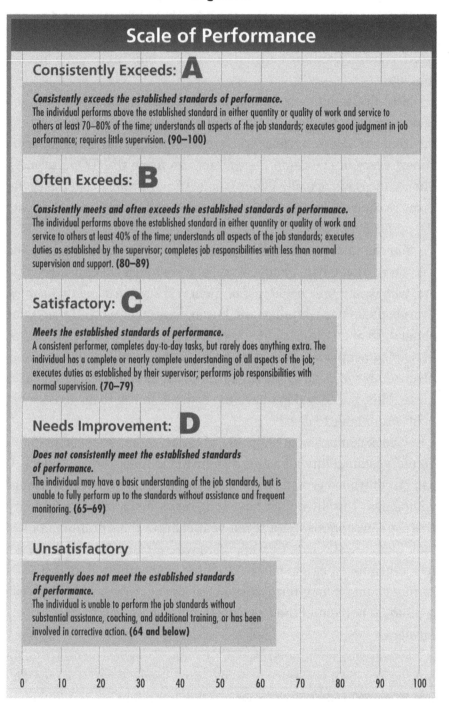

Scale of Performance

Consistently Exceeds: A

Consistently exceeds the established standards of performance.
The individual performs above the established standard in either quantity or quality of work and service to others at least 70–80% of the time; understands all aspects of the job standards; executes good judgment in job performance; requires little supervision. **(90–100)**

Often Exceeds: B

Consistently meets and often exceeds the established standards of performance.
The individual performs above the established standard in either quantity or quality of work and service to others at least 40% of the time; understands all aspects of the job standards; executes duties as established by the supervisor; completes job responsibilities with less than normal supervision and support. **(80–89)**

Satisfactory: C

Meets the established standards of performance.
A consistent performer, completes day-to-day tasks, but rarely does anything extra. The individual has a complete or nearly complete understanding of all aspects of the job; executes duties as established by their supervisor; performs job responsibilities with normal supervision. **(70–79)**

Needs Improvement: D

Does not consistently meet the established standards of performance.
The individual may have a basic understanding of the job standards, but is unable to fully perform up to the standards without assistance and frequent monitoring. **(65–69)**

Unsatisfactory

Frequently does not meet the established standards of performance.
The individual is unable to perform the job standards without substantial assistance, coaching, and additional training, or has been involved in corrective action. **(64 and below)**

| 0 | 10 | 20 | 30 | 40 | 50 | 60 | 70 | 80 | 90 | 100 |

system. This scale differentiates the contributions people make to the organization. It defines how well and how much of the time an "A," "B, " "C," or "D" performer meets performance standards.

An average or good management team similarly affects the customer experience. Many managers hire people like them and don't consider the possible consequences. Add to this, most organizations do not effectively measure their cultures. They don't seek the voice of their people by asking such questions as "What is it like to work here? How can we improve the business?" Most companies don't have good answers for those questions. While some companies take a culture survey once or twice or three times a year, the majority do not.

"If you can't measure it, you can't improve it." Many of us are familiar with that quote. If you're not measuring your culture, maybe you're really not willing to hear the results; you're not genuinely interested. So if your customers' experiences do not consistently produce quality referrals, you might need to take another look at what your competitors are doing. Now, you may choose not to measure your culture, but it just means you're going to spend a lot more money on marketing and advertising to possibly attract new, potential customers.

Stuck on Average

A substantial number of leaders running businesses of any size—small, mid-size, or large—often operate on a kind of cruise control or autopilot. They employ a certain, basic skill set to keep the business functioning and moderately successful. But it takes a different set of skills to grow a business strategically over time and make it sustainable.

They don't know how to take it to the next level. If they did, they would do it. They're really not growing their business, they're stuck at a plateau size. They may be a stagnant company producing $50 million in revenue for the last five or 10 years, give or take $3 or $4 million. They need a breakthrough. Yet they don't know how to take it to $100 million. Why are they staying stuck? I've said it repeatedly throughout my career: A business will never outperform its leadership team.

When Keith McFarland was writing his book *The Breakthrough*

Company, he studied 1,000 of the fastest growing businesses in America. He identified nine companies that were outperforming their competition by three to one. They were in the same industry, facing the same challenges, in the same economy. And he found something rather astonishing: There were a few common practices among those nine companies, including making use of outside experts, a term McFarland called "scaffolding." The companies hired an outside expert for a specific project or task, and when they were done, their scaffold left with them. Those nine companies used experts better than their competitors.

Here are a few examples of effectively using outside experts:

☐ You're running a $25 million printing company and you'd like to get it ready to sell in three to five years. You could hire a business valuation expert to give you a true, honest assessment of what your business is worth today, and insight as to the specific areas you need to improve to increase its value as much as possible.

☐ You want to expand your brand presence in your market. You could hire a public relations firm or a branding expert to help you improve the image and effectiveness of your marketing collateral by boosting your brand.

☐ You want to improve your Internet marketing presence. You could call a company with expertise in the area of Internet marketing.

☐ You'd like to build an internal leadership development system for your current leaders and your next generation of leaders. You could consult with somebody like the author of this book.

Unwilling to Ask for a Lifeline

As I mentioned in the Preface, 70 percent of company leaders are not only uninterested in new ideas, they seem unwilling to go outside of their companies and find those experts who can come in and help their organizations gain the skills and competencies that their current executive team members lack. Whether you call it their ego or closed-mindedness, they do not even think of going outside of their own organizations to find experts who can help them build and execute a sustainable growth plan. What's worse, they don't even recognize the need for outside help. To some degree, that's understandable. They grew their business to its current state, so they obviously possess the skills and the leadership required to have taken it from where it was 10 years ago to where it is today. However, the mindset of being "good" will become a limitation for future growth. Do you ever wonder why more than 90 percent of all businesses seem to grow to a certain level of sales and then plateau and stall?

Thus, leaders are faced with a dilemma. On one hand they say they'd like to grow and improve profits and margins and shareholder value. On the other hand, they aren't really willing to do what it takes to make that happen.

It's clear that many company leaders talk about developing what they consider their most valuable asset, people, but their budget and actions do not match their words. And that's why in every industry there are only a few companies that are exceptional, the best of the best. Therefore, it stands to reason that average companies delivering "average" services or products will not differentiate themselves in the marketplace. And they will experience average customer loyalty, which means average profits, which means they will stay, if they are lucky, an average performer in their industry. But remember, that is a choice.

We'll get into more specific solutions and actions later in this book. For now, let me just say that if you're serious about countering the stagnation due to the factors just mentioned, you should assess your entire management team and then make a commitment to change and to bringing in an outside resource to help your company accomplish that goal. Determining if you have the right management team is key, because anything you do with the wrong players is going to produce limited results. You should at least know if you have a team full of keepers. How valuable would it be to shift from "I think" to "I know"? This directly impacts market share, profitability, and employee turnover, because really top talent does not like working in average companies. They stay only until they land something with a great company.

Over time, average, middle-of-the-pack companies end up with average, middle-of-the-pack performance. Extra incentive forms of compensation, such as bonuses, stock shares, and profit sharing all must be paid for. If your company is average, you may not be able to afford those kinds of bonus plans.

"Most notably, our analysis demonstrated that there are five key culture metrics which drive 14–17% higher financial performance: collaboration, job satisfaction, employee engagement, professional growth and development, and alignment with organizational values."
—Human Capital Institute Research & PS Culture Matters, 2013

Achieving Sustainable Growth

There are only a few ways you can compete in today's market: with your product or service, how well you deliver that product or service, and/or price. Whenever possible, I want my clients to be priced as one of the most expensive in their industries and to be service leaders. It all begins with the right management team, which will often translate into increased market share. By now you may be thinking the formula to long-term success is more complex than simply developing a great management team. Let me calm your blood pressure—you are correct. However, your foundation for that formula for long-term growth is very strong leadership.

Industry leading companies have executives who have figured this out. The financial performance of a business is oftentimes simply a reflection of its management team. Those with sustainable growth almost invariably have management teams that are significantly above average. I'm not talking about just top management here, I mean frontline supervisors and team leaders as well.

One indication of the quality of your culture and leaders is employee turnover. Companies that attend to developing talent and a great workplace culture—not to win awards, but to make their employees happy and successful—do not have turnover problems. In fact, they have people waiting in line to work there. When they announce two openings, they'll receive 1,500 résumés. They get to select only the best of the best.

Profits and market share can be either flat, declining, or growing, or some combination of all three. If they aren't growing, that means company leaders haven't figured out how to achieve sustainability yet. Their profitability chart looks more like that EKG. Industry leaders do not experience those dramatic spikes and dips. Exceptional companies even do well during industry downturns.

Depending on whose research you believe, it takes between three and seven years to significantly change a workplace culture. It takes time to get everybody on board, to get everybody rowing in the same direction. It takes time to weed out the bad apples. It takes time to attract new, top talent to replace them and integrate the new people into your culture.

It also takes time to develop your management team and start training your frontline associates before they "get it." Keep in mind that when you start measuring employee engagement and culture, it takes time to implement action plans based on the results of those surveys. Managers need to collaborate with frontline associates to put action plans in place, and for those plans to work their way up through an organization one improvement at a time. Then the culture begins to improve.

When I was working at one of the top healthcare systems in Michigan, I was in charge of all the training and leadership development. To begin to address a nurse retention problem, one of the strategies we decided to use was to conduct culture surveys every six months, and we decided to add accountability so that managers would take action planning seriously. We trained our 500-member management team in how to share the survey results and how to collaborate with their staff and design improvements with the team's input. In addition, 20 percent of every manager's performance review focused on whether they measurably improved at least one action item from the employee survey. We believed if we could get 500 managers doing that across the company, we would substantially improve the culture for the entire system, and that improves the quality of care being delivered. Our new leadership core training curriculum and our new accountability system also significantly contributed to our culture change movement. Four years after we launched that work, this healthcare organization won the Best Place to Work in Detroit award, and the organization was saving millions annually in turnover costs.

Even top companies need to stay vigilant and keep applying these practices. It's tempting to get complacent after two, three, four years at the top. But it's a dangerous assumption for a CEO to think that the competition is going to continue to act next year like it did this year. What happens if they don't? What happens if two of your competitors figure this out and make that commitment to develop their management team far faster than you do?

CHAPTER 2

How Is Your Current Leadership Team Impacting Your Business?

---

*My job is **not** to be easy on people. My job is to make them
better ... And to take these great people we have and to
push them and make them even better, coming up with more
aggressive visions of how it **could** be.*

—Steve Jobs, Apple

On February 5, 2012, the New York Giants played the New England
Patriots in the Super Bowl. The Giants won 21-17. It marked five of
the last 10 years the Patriots had made it to the coveted game. But
what's really interesting about this contest is that the Giants had 11
players on their roster who had never even been drafted; the Patriots
had 18 who were never drafted either, which makes 29 individuals
who were not drafted by anyone, or were not signed to an NFL contract. Yet the coaching staffs on these two teams saw the potential and
developed these 29 players to contribute.

Those are just two examples of organizations with senior level
leaders and coaches who are exceptional at spotting potential and
developing talent. What was it about the owners, general manager,
and coaching staffs of those two teams that enabled them to spot the
potential in those 29 individuals?

You should ask yourself as well, "How are we developing talent? Do we have the right people on our team?" For many, the answer too often is "I have no idea."

Here's another question for you: What do Joe Montana, Brett Favre, Albert Pujols, Wayne Gretzky, and Miguel Cabrera have in common? They're all going to be in the Hall of Fame, or are already there. These men are great athletes, the best of the best in their particular sport. And all five of them at some point in their careers have been cut, fired, traded, or had contracts not renewed. How can this be, if they're so good? It was because some leader had the courage to say, "This person doesn't fit the future direction of our team or our company." Most leaders do not have the courage to make such tough staffing decisions. They worry too much about their own careers and egos, or they're so close with some of their direct reports that they won't let them go. You simply cannot have a management team with 50-60 percent of your managers being "C" performers.

So when you talk about signs and symptoms of weak leadership and poor service, one of the ways to measure that (we'll be talking about measurement a lot in this book) has to do with customer loyalty, and how many times people buy a product or service from your company over and over again. Customer loyalty is a big indicator of how well your culture is working for you. And the number and quality of your referrals is another strong indicator.

How hard it is to attract top talent? That's another sign of leadership problems. Do great employees want to work for your company? How do you know they're great? There are other parts of the business that are indicators, too. By the way, how do you quantify who is a top performer? You can monitor cash flow. You can also monitor how well the business is doing profitabilitywise. With our one-page scorecard system, you can monitor any size of company, once you decide which KPIs are critical to monitor. The danger for each leader reading this book is that you're probably thinking that you're doing a very good job of communicating how the business is performing, and 90 percent of you are not. I can prove it in less than five minutes.

What happens is, over time, at different levels in the organization, you end up with too many people in leadership positions who are at best . . . average performers. If you fill the leadership of an organization with average talent and a few above-average performers, that's the kind of culture you're going to produce, and those are the business results you're going to get, but remember, that is a management decision. You're also going to get customer loyalty that is a reflection of that mediocre talent. Without tools for spotting and then developing talent, you inevitably wind up with too many average performers in leadership positions.

The cost of finding, hiring, and training each new employee is 1.5 times his/her annual salary.
    —**Marcus Buckingham and Curt Coffman, *First, Break All the Rules***

People Like to Follow a Great Leader

When all is said and done, great leaders simply trust their people and assemble great teams. Then they inspire these people and give them freedom to perform at their best. People want to work with a great leader. They'll gladly follow without being told to.

A study conducted by *Psychology Bulletin* showed that the output of average workers is 48 percent greater than that of non-producers. And the output of superior workers is 48 percent more than that of average producers. When you look at the productivity, or the output of people in management, and you wonder why your business isn't performing at a higher level, you need to ask yourself if you have the right leaders in the job. Part of what we're challenging here is why executives tolerate their current, average leadership teams and then question why their businesses aren't performing better.

In their book, *The Customer Experience Revolution*, Jeofrey Bean and Sean Van Tyne quote the top 10 customer experience leaders. According to their research, those leaders generated cumulative total returns that were 41 percent better than the Standard & Poor's

500 Index. In the 1990s, McKinsey & Company reported in the book *The War for Talent* that high-performing individuals or leaders generate between 48 and 129 percent higher revenue than average performers.

According to the 2013 *Harvard Business Review* article "What 'A' Players Bring to the Table," about the proof of return on investment training, the **best developer** at Apple is at least <u>nine</u> times as productive as the average software engineer at other technology companies, while the **best blackjack dealer** at Caesars Palace in Las Vegas keeps his table playing at least <u>five</u> times as long as the average dealer on the strip. If that's not enough proof, the **best sales associate** at Nordstrom sells at least <u>eight</u> times as much as the average sales associate at other department stores. And the **best transplant surgeon** at a top-notch medical clinic has a success rate at least <u>six</u> times that of the average transplant surgeon. These examples should force you to rethink your decisions about budgeting for developing leaders and training for associates.

Every employee in your company, every single day, has discretionary effort that they can choose to put forth or not. They can go a little above and beyond their job duties or not. They can come back from lunch and get back to work, or they can stand around and talk about their plans for the evening or yesterday's game on TV. What if you could get 5 or 10 percent extra effort from 30 or 40 percent of your organization? That's the equivalent of hiring 10 or 20 new employees without adding to the fixed expense.

Too many managers don't understand how to get this kind of additional productivity out of a large percentage of their current workforce. When profits flounder, they tend to go back to traditional, old ways of improving profits, which is slashing expenses and often laying off staff. Then they wonder why morale is down. And it doesn't solve the problem. You cannot have a high-performing company producing great financial results—with incredible customer loyalty from great customer experiences—in a place where morale is mediocre at best.

So why do executives tolerate less than top performers? Why aren't more executives assessing and developing their management teams? As I see it, remember, they have the following choices:

1. Accept their leadership team as it is

2. Work with an executive search firm to recruit and pay for new leadership talent

3. Develop the talent they have

4. A combination of numbers two and three

If they choose to develop their current talent, which in combination with the second option above is what great companies do, they need to begin with an assessment. And from a strategic standpoint, if you're going to spend time and company money and resources to develop your leadership talent, you need to understand how to do that.

A Square Peg for a Square Hole

In his book *How the Mighty Fall*, author Jim Collins shared a question he was once asked: "If you were to pick one marker above all others as a warning sign that your company may be on the decline, may be getting ready to implode, what would it be?" His answer? "It would be the declining proportion of key seats filled by the right people now and for the future."

So at the end of the day, if you're wondering why your organization isn't producing and delivering compared to your competition, I suggest that you don't have the right quality talent in those key seats. Do you even know what the key seats are in your organization? Do you have the right people in them? How would you even quantify the right people, based on your performance review process? We'll get more into how you assess your leadership talent later on. For now, let's just say most organizations do not have an effective process for assessing performance, or a great system for developing great leaders.

When you study management teams in most companies, you will tend to see a pretty traditional bell curve. You will always find a large percentage—often 50-60 percent of the bell curve—to be average "C" performers. There will also be some poor performers, meaning some small percentage of "Ds," people who are simply not producers. And finally, you'll see the rock stars, the "As," the superior performers, plus a percentage of "B" performers that frequently go above and beyond delivering results. Without revealing actual company names, in more than 80 percent of the companies I have visited or worked with, their management team's distribution looks similar to what I've just described.

A performers	10%
B performers	20%
C performers	60%
D and below performers	10%

If you're going to develop people into great leaders, based on my experience, the process should be very intentional. To develop them to perform at higher levels, it helps to be able to move from saying, "I think Bob can be a great leader" to "I *know* Bob can be a great leader." Exactly how do you go from thinking Bob will be a great leader to *knowing* it as you consider talent development? First, you must assess Bob's potential for leadership development and decide who will do the assessment.

Again, when I talk about leadership, regardless of the size of the organization, there are three levels I'm referring to: senior leaders/executives, which can mean different things in different companies; middle management, typically department heads and directors; and frontline managers/supervisors, which includes team leaders. It doesn't matter which research or articles you read, it's not the experience, college degrees, or other factors that determine whether your manager is a high performer. What matters far more is the fit. Is this person right for the job? That's where assessments are so critical. It does beg the question: Do you have an accurate description of each manager's position regarding what you are looking for—the qualities, the skills, the behaviors?

I believe there are core leadership competencies and behaviors that every leader must possess, and that they can be assessed and developed. When you use statistically valid assessment tools, it's like taking an MRI or a CAT scan of every leader in your organization. There are many great assessment tools that can help company leaders develop leadership talent at all three of those leadership levels. However, most leaders do not get accurate feedback. Most leaders do not get effective coaching. And most leaders do not have a very well thought out, strategic individual development plan, or IDP.

Research tells us that people leave managers, not companies. So much money has been thrown at the challenge of keeping good people—when, in the end, turnover is mostly a manager issue. If you have a turnover problem, look first to your managers.

—Marcus Buckingham and Curt Coffman, *First, Break All the Rules*

Growing Companies Understand Leadership and Culture

A few years ago, my company partnered with the University of South Florida to create an executive round table event as part of launching the Innisbrook Leadership Institute. Held at Innisbrook Resort in Tampa, we invited hundreds of executives from around Southwest Florida to our round table. We asked them questions and they replied using an audience response system. We asked them what's important to them. One question, which I've asked many times, is: "When you go on vacation, what can you not stop thinking about?" I usually get the same answers, and did in this round table. They worry about improving the quality of their staff/talent, getting more customers, and increasing cash flow.

Consider those three factors for a moment. The problem is not the economy, because the companies that are growing in this economy have figured out what type of leadership is required, the kind of culture that needs to be built, and they understand their customers' needs and wants not only for today, but for the future. In addition, they're always assessing their organization. They have a process improvement mentality, always looking for ways to make it better.

Here's a quick test you can take any time. Go for a walk and ask the first four or five manager-level staff members you see, "What are the company's top three priorities?" Ninety-eight percent of the time, they will not be able to accurately answer with specifics. If you follow up with the question "What are the top three priorities that you are being held accountable for and have discussed with your boss or put in writing?", about 90 percent also will have no reply. And you wonder why your margins, your quality, and/or possibly your productivity of staff are not higher. Who should be responsible for these disappointing answers?

If you don't have alignment with the key priorities of the business, and you don't have the right leadership team to run and grow your business, your success will plateau and/or suffer. More than likely, your competition will take market share from you. If you don't have everybody on the same page, if you don't have organizational alignment, how would you possibly expect to execute at a high level? Without a strategy in place, without alignment, your business results are simply luck. I don't find wishing and dreaming and luck to be very good business strategies. People need systems and processes to be effective.

Most privately owned businesses with less than 1,000 in staff are not as disciplined with processes and systems as they need to be. If you study some of the great franchises of the world, whether it's McDonald's or Subway, or any of the others, they're very effective businesses. This is not because their food is great. If you look at the management of a McDonald's, it's often a 65-year-old who's come back to work part time because their 401(k) is in the tank, and the employees are 15- to 16-year-old kids who can't even make their beds in the morning. Yet they're running multibillion dollar operations.

If you can read and follow the systems, you could run a McDonald's effectively tomorrow. Those same systems and processes are what's missing in most businesses. I believe most leaders either don't have the courage, have ego problems, or they refuse to get outside experts to help them assess their management teams and establish systems to strategically develop the current and future leaders of their organization.

The Four-Letter Words to Avoid for Real Company Growth

Two four-letter words that I mock all the time are "good" and "busy." People will tell me, "John, we're good. Look at what we've done. We've had 4 to 7 percent growth three years in a row. We've come out of the recession." And on and on. They'll brag about what's supposedly going on in their organization, and how "busy" they are.

Yet when you look at their budget, they have no systematic approach for developing their current and future leaders. And they wonder why they have to spend so much money on marketing, promotion, advertising, and public relations. They don't get that many referrals from their existing customers because there's nothing to brag about.

Think about the term *discretionary effort*. If your organization has a lot of employees, let's pick some round number and say 1,000, your organization will typically look like that bell curve I described earlier. About half of your organization, from what I see most of the time, is made up of average or below performers. By now you might be wondering what would be different if you could move some percentage of those "C" performers back to being "B" performers.

I highly recommend you have a system to quantify talent in your current organization. The sad truth is, most of the time you'll have just as many "A" performers as you will "D" and below performers. Why so many "Ds"? What would be different if there were no "Ds," and those new, open positions were filled with "B" performers? The morale and energy in your company would significantly change for the better. Oftentimes, many of those average "C" performers were not hired that way, either; something happened to convert them over time to simply showing up, doing their job, and going home. What is it about your culture and the way your current leaders manage your company that drains the energy and excitement from these individuals? Your culture will trump your strategy every time.

If you want to change the performance of your business, you need to assess your leadership team and begin to systematically make sure that a.) you have the right people on the team and b.) you begin to develop them. When we talk about *leadership development*, the definition starts with an executive decision to assess and develop *anyone* in a leadership position. This needs to be done repetitively over years, since people continue to grow.

Of course, it's based on the premise that you understand the demands and the responsibilities associated with each leadership position and that you've actually spent time documenting their responsibilities. Then you create a budget to fund that development because you've decided that the future of your company is going to be a reflection of your management team. You also decide to stop tolerating some average or okay performers in leadership positions because that type of performer is likely to cause turnover. Remember, employees do not leave companies, they leave managers, and there's plenty of data to prove it.

CHAPTER 3

What Would Your Company Look Like as an Industry Leader?

Build a place where ordinary people...can do extraordinary things.
—**Keith R. McFarland,** *The Breakthrough Company*

We've talked about the top 8 percent of elite businesses and some steps you can take to join them at that level. Examples help bring that picture into focus. During my career, I've worked with two very different companies that achieved what we're talking about in this book: Ford Motor Company and Oakwood Healthcare System. They are what you could call "models," one manufacturing and one healthcare.

Ford Motor Company's Romeo Engine Plant in Romeo, Michigan, began as a tractor facility. Today, the Romeo Engine Plant is considered one of the top, premier manufacturing facilities in the world, and its culture is driving its phenomenal success. That success is the result of a comprehensive strategy to build the best 4.6L engines in the world.

Oakwood Healthcare, which operates healthcare facilities all over Southeastern Michigan, was having difficulty retaining highly qualified employees. With a dedicated plan and follow-through, in just a few years the health system was not only turned around dramatically, it was recognized as a great place to work. The smaller your company, the faster your turnaround can take place.

Building a World-Class Engine

Located about 50 miles north of Detroit, for many years Ford's Romeo Engine Plant built tractors, 10,000 annually until about 1984. That's when Ford decided to phase out tractor production. Around 1987, the doors were closed and locked for the last time, and the more than 2,000 unionized employees were laid off. Ford leaders wanted to replace the tractor operation with new, high-tech, modular engines. So Ford management first collaborated with the United Auto Workers (UAW) and selected two or three key leaders to head up this massive transition and changeover. They made a conscious decision that they were going to reopen the plant in an updated facility. Moreover, they didn't want the new operation to continue with the current, long-standing manufacturing mentality: They decided to create a new culture.

Ford recognized the importance of zero quality defects, so they did some research and benchmarking while the concrete was being removed and repoured in the factory's floors and all the old equipment was removed. A team of UAW leaders and executive team members spent several months studying the best of the best companies across America. They were set on making auto industry history by doing things very differently. It was essentially an experiment, and Romeo was to be a pilot plant.

By the early 1990s, Ford settled on a plan to make the reconditioned plant part manufacturing and part machining facility. The company was going to run it using a team approach in a way that would secure jobs and offer customers a better product. In partnership with the UAW, Ford leaders put together a new contract: They would establish a zero defects philosophy inside the plant. And they kept that philosophy in mind as they put the finishing touches on the new operation.

For example, this Ford-UAW leadership team determined that there should be no classes of people in the plant. You shouldn't know if somebody dresses nicer or drives a bigger car or parks in a special parking place. They did away with the management dining room, replacing it with just one where everybody would eat the same food. They got rid of management reserved parking places; if you got there

36

late, you got a bad parking spot.

The team also decided that everyone would dress the same. When I arrived at the plant in 1993 as the team consultant on-site, we all wore the same uniform: navy-blue, cotton pants; a brass belt buckle; and a light-blue, short-sleeved shirt with our name embroidered on the pocket. From secretaries to frontline managers, to floor sweepers and engineers, we all dressed the same. So when you walked through the facility and you passed somebody in the hallway, and on their shirt it would read "George," you would say, "Hi, George," and George would reply, "Hi, John."

Ford took ego and class out of the equation when it came to their employees. The company announced, "This is going to be one plant where we're all in this together." And they meant it.

At the same time, they took other equalizing measures. They did away with time clocks. They abolished the role of the assembly line foremen, so workers didn't have to worry about foremen write-ups, if they were late. They put buttons around the plant. Any one of the 2,000 employees could hit one of those buttons and stop the assembly line. Leaders wanted employees to feel ownership in the quality of the product that went past their assembly station. A core training curriculum was designed and rolled out for all employees, with courses taught by both UAW and management associates.

In July 1988, Ford unveiled details about the two engines to be built at the plant, and they introduced new quality and inspection methods. They hung billboard-sized monitors to show how close they were to various targets and track any quality problems. If something happened in the plant, people were paged immediately.

In short, Ford created an atmosphere where every associate treated the plant as if they were one of its owners. Training and development became a priority. The associates were required to take 300 hours of ongoing training and development. A new curriculum offered courses on subjects such as quality, problem solving, team concepts, and productivity.

The leadership team created a UAW-management steering committee that met every Monday. I was one of the facilitators of those meetings. Plant issues were discussed, but not in a UAW versus management way. Everyone's perspective focused on how to improve the quality of engines made at this plant. Their goal—everyone's articulated, share goal—was to produce the highest-quality engine in the history of the auto industry. That's what the mission statement made clear: "The purpose of the Romeo Engine Plant is to produce the highest-quality production engine in the world that meets all of our customers' requirements at a cost lower than the competition, and to develop teams of employees who are the best engine builders in the world."

The workplace revolution continued. Flexible work assignments were created. The number of labor and skilled trades classifications were reduced. The typical plant might have as many as 200 labor classifications and as many as eight skilled trades classifications, however, the Romeo plant ended up with just 11 labor classifications and two skilled trades classifications. Every single day, everything we did in that facility targeted making it simpler, faster, and more productive, and every single associate focused on that goal.

The entire facility was organized into 13 work teams that were responsible for their own safety, quality, productivity, and equipment maintenance. That meant the same people were responsible for production *and* quality. Every team had a budget and received a weekly report on estimated upcoming expenses. They shared responsibility for those expenses with all other teams. So if your team members left the lights on over the weekend, it impacted your team's weekly scorecard. Bottom line, teams were responsible for their own expenses and overall success.

As time went on, we employed the very visible and effective use of what's called "scoreboarding." We'll get more into this tool later, but briefly, inside the Ford Motor Company plant was a giant, hanging scorecard. It looked like the scoreboard in the end zone of a football stadium. It was neon and changed by the minute. There were small neon signs around the plant letting people know where they were at on their production, if there was a problem, and so on. We also kept score regarding training and development, and produced reports about who was attending the training classes and who was not.

There is much more, but you get the idea. It's no surprise that within a few years, this plant won the Ward's Automotive Engine of the Year award, which is an enormous, prestigious award in that industry.

The Romeo Engine Plant had an entire 90-day period where the engines being produced did not have *one* quality defect—zero defects for 90 days. Not one engine was returned to a dealership anywhere in the United States. A Ford engine plant had never accomplished that before.

By 1996, about five years after it was opened, that plant was producing more than 800,000 engines a year. Eventually, we had to assemble a team of people to respond to all the requests from around the world for benchmarking trips. They wanted to know "How are you being able to do this? How could you take a traditional culture and make such an incredible turnaround in just four years?"

This plant was also the subject of a case study in the *Harvard Business Review.* It all started with a vision and a joint partnership between management and the UAW. It wasn't just a management philosophy, they lived it; it was the way they ran the business.

What we found was that the average company today doesn't have a clue what people are capable of.

—Keith R. McFarland, *The Breakthrough Company*

Happier Employees, Better Care

Around 2001, not long after I left Ford, I accepted a director level position at Oakwood Healthcare. The healthcare industry in Southeastern Michigan back in 2001 was challenged. There weren't enough nurses in general, so Sunday newspaper ads offering $5,000 signing bonuses were not uncommon.

The executive team at Oakwood Healthcare decided to take on the goal of developing the current and future leaders in their organization. My role was to lead a new department. I was responsible for physician training and education, initiating culture improvement processes, leadership development activities, and training and development for all employees.

The company owned four hospitals and several satellite locations, with about 10,000 employees and a 500-member management team. Up until that point, there never had been any systematic approach for developing leaders, so we created a core training curriculum to define what it meant to be a leader at Oakwood Healthcare. We initiated change and began with leadership training. Then we added an assessment component to identify what leadership competencies our current leaders needed to acquire.

At first, not everybody was committed to taking the training courses, so we designed a new and improved performance appraisal process. We modeled it after the one used by Jack Welch and General Electric at the time. There were three fundamental components to that process, for which every leader was responsible:

1. The results and measurable targets that they were supposed to deliver
2. The commitment to talk about and demonstrate the behaviors and values of the organization
3. Individual development

Every single manager in the organization, all 500 from the CEO on down to an afternoon shift team leader, was also responsible for their individual development plan (IDP). Part of that plan required that all leaders attend the core leadership training, from the CEO down. One of our goals was to ensure that any leader could look across the room and see a vice president learning the same coaching skill, or a team leader could participate in a classroom training exercise on trust with directors and managers. Those managers who were already more skillful became great mentors in the leadership classroom experiences.

As we got a little bit further down the path, we started measuring culture using a culture engagement survey. In order to get all 500 leaders accountable for taking action based on the survey results, we spent a significant amount of time upfront in education and communication throughout the organization. We also built into our accountability system for managers that every manager, with their team, had to decide on one area identified in the survey they would improve upon before the next survey was taken. This added accountability to the process. We determined if we could get 500 managers to improve one aspect of something important to their team, that would create significant movement within the organization in 12 months. We did that year after year.

In the second year, we put a leadership scorecard in place. We decided to take accountability for the entire organization to a whole new level. Not only did we create an organizational scorecard that could be captured on one page, we could break it down by teams, functional units, hospital, or location. So keeping score began to really make a difference. We'll share more about this scorecard method in Chapter 7. As a result, a few leaders were moved out of leadership positions and back into other jobs where they were a better fit within the system. We also began to improve hiring or promoting new leaders in the organization, and we began to take a much more strategic approach to developing current leaders.

In the third year there, we recognized the organization had not targeted the development of future leaders, and that bench strength and succession planning were important for the company's future. We defined *bench strength* as a system of identifying pools of people/talent who, with specific development, could serve the organization at one or two levels above their current position. We strategically stated that our bench of future talent would always have people who were ready and waiting to fill positions. So we launched a future leaders high-potential program. We created an application process whereby people could either submit their names or be nominated by a vice president or director-level person. Following an application, the applicant faced a hiring and selection committee.

Ultimately, we ended up with 16 people in a one-year program focused on expediting their development as the next generation of executives. We set up a one-day assessment center with an outside consulting firm to help us. At that time, we used the Hogan Leadership Assessment Tool. We were working in partnership with a great national research group called The Advisory Board, in Washington, D.C., and using some of their assessment tools. We also started conducting some leadership 360 Surveys within the organization, gathering feedback from everyone around those company leaders. The idea was to learn how the leaders' behaviors were perceived by their managers, their peers, and their direct reports, and whether their staff would go above and beyond for them.

Leaders in that program began to develop themselves more strategically. They even had an executive coach working with them during that period. The entire program was really focused on expediting their development. What was occurring during those three years was that we were creating a culture where every individual throughout the organization would have the opportunity to grow and develop to be their absolute best.

During the leadership development one-year program, the return on investment of their project to the organization had to be at least $1 better than the cost of the one-year leadership development program for each participant. If the cost for each leader in the program was $20,000, and there were four on a team, that project had to bring in a return on investment of at least $80,001 that was measurable and signed off on by the CFO. All four groups significantly surpassed their final ROI, making the entire one-year program FREE to the organization.

Throughout the 12 months of this future leaders program, team members were learning how to collaborate with people they may not have worked closely with before. We were teaching them to measure results, quantify their existence in the program, and remain focused on their team's project delivery and ROI.

We created a company-wide leadership scorecard at Oakwood

Healthcare. This scorecard could be broken down for departments, a particular hospital, or even a team. On a single piece of paper, we identified the 10 most important measures of what it means to be a leader. We also created a color-coded chart to gauge people's scores.

Going through all of these measures at Oakwood, we were designing a self-sustaining program that paid for itself over time. And as we began developing great leaders, we improved our trust in management factor. Within 36 months of launching what I've just described, organizational trust in management was up 89 percent, employee satisfaction was up 46 percent, employee turnover was reduced 31 percent, and communication between different work teams and work shifts improved 62 percent. This not only saved the organization several million dollars a year, it helped attract nurses and easily retain those already in our system.

Many healthcare organizations suffer from high turnover, which obviously impacts the quality of care. We fixed that. Within a few years, Oakwood won Best Place to Work awards. And the entire process of developing leaders allowed Oakwood to deliver a much higher quality of care to its customers (its patients and physicians) while improving the culture and financial performance of the entire organization.

The most important corporate resource over the next 20 years will be talent. Even as the demand for talent goes up, the supply of it will be going down.
—Ed Michaels, Helen Handfeld-Jones, and Beth Axelrod,
The War for Talent

How Companies Become the "Best of the Best"

Implementing a culture change model starts with that all-important executive decision to be the best. So right upfront, it requires a different level of commitment and decision-making by executives. Then, those at the top need to create a vision for what this business could look like in 5 to 10 years. They would see the power of having effective leadership, and the right talent and systems in an organization. When they study or think about processes and systems, they would recognize that they don't want to reinvent the wheel, so they would benchmark other great companies, meaning those who are already the best.

Then they would decide what type of culture they want to build: it's very defined and well-articulated, and very intentional. What kind of people, what kind of talent are they going to need to be exceptional? What kind of ongoing training and development will be necessary to ensure that they have world-class talent? You can't fill an organization with mediocre talent and expect exceptional results, so training, coaching, and development are essential components of your long-term success.

Another component is measurement and accountability. People need to know the score, so measurement and accountability play a big role in the model. Creating the right culture also involves continuous improvement, while allowing people to grow and develop to be their best.

There is the leadership aspect as well, with some sort of engagement structure needed. Typically, an organization that wants to become world-class will put together a steering committee of anywhere from five to eight associates at a variety of levels in the organization to head up this culture change movement.

The final component of the model would be to have an actual plan to strategically take the business to the next level over the next five years. Not a business plan in a binder that you submit to a bank, but a strategic plan that's well thought out and can be articulated to every associate.

We'll get further into the details of the "blueprint" for culture change in Chapter 5, but this is the basis of that model.

CHAPTER 4

What Defines a Great Leader?

Only one significant factor distinguished the upper quartile of successful managers from the lower quartile of unsuccessful managers—caring.

—Center for Creative Leadership

Who is the greatest manager or boss you've ever worked for as an adult? Bring that person to mind right now. And what about those not so great bosses? The difference between those two types of bosses likely had little to do with their skill set; it was all in how they behaved. In this chapter, we're going to define great leadership. But before we do, what are two words that describe that great boss, the greatest leader you've ever worked for? Write them down here:

_____ _____

During the course of my career, I've asked probably as many as 10,000 people in audiences around the country that question. The way they answer says a great deal about the unique combination of qualities that make up great leaders. They never talk about what I call technical skills or competencies. People never say things such as "She was a great doctor," "He was a great engineer," "She was a great attorney," or "He was a great designer." Whether they work at Subway,

Payless Shoes, or a Toyota dealership, they all use similar, more emotional descriptions. Here are some words in Figure 4 that define great leaders through the eyes of employees at all levels across America.

Figure 4

How Employees Describe Great Leaders

Ethical Personable **Caring** Motivational
FOCUSED **Inspiring Loyal** Composed
Energetic *Problem Solver* **Tolerant**
Compassionate Collaborative HONEST
Dependable Trusting Mentor **Smart**
Hard Working Respectful *Visionary*
Teacher Consistent **Resilient Thankful**
Confident Knowledge **Accountable**
Supportive *Passionate* Develops Others
CHARISMATIC **Listens Driven** Appreciative

Source: Premier Executive Forums

58% say that they work for a "bad boss"
82% say they don't have enough impact on the bottom line (constrained by boss)
80% say they will leave if they have a good opportunity
        —**McKinsey Study of 650 executives and board members**

The Truth about Leadership

What does it mean to lead? What makes a great leader? Well, that can depend on whom you ask. If you want my one-sentence definition, a great leader gets work done through others. I see a great leader as someone who has the ability to influence others in a positive manner. You may have your own definition, and that's okay. I'm not saying mine is the only definition. There are probably thousands of definitions. The famous management consultant Dr. W. Edwards Deming would have had a different definition. Colin Powell might have a different definition. Nearly everyone has their own definition.

But I think we can agree that leaders who are the "best of the best" influence people in such a positive manner that they affect work getting done, and those leaders don't have to do it themselves, they delegate effectively and have a very positive "impact" on the entire organization. That's true about great leadership at any level. We could be talking about a vice president or a nurse manager on the afternoon shift in a hospital. We could be talking about it in any number of businesses. The focus is on the impact leaders have.

As you consider how much priority leadership development should have in your company, I invite you to take a good look at what I call "Leadership Impact Truths." Based on my 30 years of experience and the research of other people, I've come up with a list of "truths" related to leaders who run businesses. I believe they're an important part of what defines a great leader; it is about their impact. These are truths from a 30,000-foot view. They're undeniable, and in some cases immeasurable, but they're happening in your business right now. All leaders affect the organization, in a positive manner or not. The list of leadership impact truths is really not open for negotiation in a company, and it applies to businesses across all industries and of all sizes. This list should provide an eye-opening, sobering reality check for those leaders in a company's senior positions.

As you read this list, you will likely quickly come to a conclusion or guess about how each truth is reflected in your business. Unfortunately, you are guessing. In my 30-year history, I have never been in a company that could show me the data for all 18 truths. How valuable would it be to have facts and data about your company regarding each leadership truth?

Leadership Impact Truths

1. **How leaders treat employees is how employees treat customers.**

   Exceptional service only comes from happy and engaged employees. Managers significantly impact employee morale, which in turn affects each customer's experience.

2. **You cannot win with average talent on your team.**

   The world of sports proves that only great talent wins. Great talent understands teamwork and collaboration. You may turn a profit, and yes you may run a good company, but you will never reach your company's true potential.

3. **An organization is always a reflection of its leadership.**

   Big or small, it makes no difference. Whatever a company does well is what its owners or executive team members do well, and vice versa. Their strength or weakness is the company's strength or weakness.

4. **People pay more to receive great service.**

   Look around your business community and find out which companies are the most expensive in their industries. How do they get away with charging more than their competitors? Their margins are higher and their customers expect more. But, are they really better?

5. **Employees want to know the direction in which the company is heading.**

   Consider the type of employees you want on your payroll, the first people your customers will see every day. What percentage of them put forth that extra 5 to 10 percent worth of discretionary effort every day? Do you want a company full of people who simply do their jobs every day, or enthusiastic team players who understand their roles and have bought into the company's vision and mission? They cannot do this if you do not communicate that vision and mission.

6. A leader's number one responsibility is to select top talent.
Fill a company with people who are a great fit for their key responsibilities and motivation follows. Unfortunately, too many leaders allow nonperformers to hang around. Change your hiring and selection system to only allow top talent. Every part of your business execution will improve. What would you change about your hiring process if you were forced to keep every new hire for 10 years?

7. High performers do not like working with average performers.
How many "A" or "B" performers do you have in your company? The challenge is that 90 percent of executives gather no data on this issue. Take great care with whom you surround your top performers. Remember, executive search firms call top performers regularly.

8. People always watch their boss.
Every manager, CEO, or frontline supervisor has a "brand" at work. That brand is what people say about them when they're not around. Employees know when their boss is having a bad or a great day. They watch how their boss dresses, runs meetings, and whether their boss is prompt. They even pay attention to where their boss vacations, and the type of car their boss drives. What's your leadership brand like? Remember, it impacts how people trust you.

9. Your culture is stronger than your strategy.
For a quick test, send two or three top performers to an executive conference. When they return, have them share the new ideas they bring back with their colleagues and see how it energizes and improves your existing culture, or not. Your culture stagnates when people learn and do the same things the same way for years. If you decide to change your future, you must think about how long it will take to change your culture.

10. **Seventy percent of leaders are not coachable.**

    Okay, I don't know the exact number, but my 30-plus years of developing leaders and working with entrepreneurs of mid-sized companies leads me to conclude that seven out of ten executives are not open to having outside experts help them with their business. It might be ego, or it might be simply that they have strong opinions that blind them to alternatives or growth. The consequences of this closed-minded condition are potentially hazardous.

11. **Without alignment, organizations cannot execute at a high level.**

    A five-minute tour of your company will prove this point. Ask the first six people you pass if they can articulate their top measurable priorities for the calendar year, if they have discussed and agreed to them with their bosses, and if they have a written copy of these priorities back at their desks. Rarely will you get even one positive response. Getting every associate aligned to the business priorities is critical. Without alignment, execution is simply courting Lady Luck.

12. **People like to know what is expected of them.**

    Clarity is a powerful force in the workplace. It affects whether your workplace is boring or passionate. Clarity about the values of your company, your team's performance expectations, and how each person's compensation formula will be calculated, rather than keeping these things secret and making people guess, makes a difference. The choice is yours.

13. **Top performers expect to be paid more.**

    If you knew your competition was attempting to buy two of your top five performers, what would you do immediately? The pressure to compensate top performers requires that you have a simple accountability system that allows you to quantify the performances of individuals and teams alike. Are they at risk of leaving you? Are you positive? What if you are wrong? What would it take for someone to buy them from you?

14. Employees must be able to trust their managers at every level.

Trust is an interesting dynamic in the workplace. It has a wider reach than you might expect. Can you trust your manager for honest feedback? Can you trust your manager to deal with poor performers? Can you trust your manager to build a fun place to work? Can you trust your manager to remove barriers and help you when you need assistance?

15. Employees like it when poor performers call in sick.

Poor performers are a virus in your company. They work hard to do very little and everyone knows who they are. The tone and energy of the workplace goes up two or three notches when one of your sour grapes calls in sick; it quickly becomes more positive and friendly simply because the virus is absent.

16. Create a great place to work and you will attract top talent.

Imagine the power of a magnet. That is the kind of force in play when you create a culture that employees enjoy, where they know they can grow, and is one they tell others about. Every company has a brand in the business community. Is your brand a magnet or simply nonexistent, like in most companies? Has your culture been created by design or by luck?

17. Ineffective delegation is the single biggest barrier to growth.

Delegating tasks and responsibilities requires managers to let go of certain work. It requires properly trained employees and well-designed systems. The right delegation formula links leadership, employees, and systems. All three must be effective, or delegation will not follow.

18. One hundred percent of managers lead by example.

It is a fact that associates watch their managers: the way they dress, the cars they drive, the vacations they take, what time they arrive and leave every day, and so on. Each of your managers has a brand at work. I describe your brand as what people say about you when you're not around. Are your managers and executives setting the right example? What percentage of your existing management team would you rehire? Do they consistently demonstrate your company's values? Is your current leadership development system producing the right managers? Is it producing a brand of managers that sends the right message? How do you know?

Do you agree that these truths I just outlined are important? I would encourage you to take a hard look at any points with which you disagree. Based on my professional experience with scores of the world's best organizations, these principles apply to every business, with very few exceptions. The primary reason I put together these leadership truths is that not everyone has had the opportunity to spend time inside a great company. Understandably, some leaders like evidence that certain precepts work. That's why, throughout this book, you'll find that I share other experts' research and statistics, as well as my own, for further validation.

High performers generate 48–129% higher revenue than average performers.

—McKinsey War on Talent Survey

Core Leadership Behaviors

Remember the quote "Your actions speak so loud I cannot hear a word you are saying?" Every leader in your company has a personal brand, which oftentimes is formed by actions and behaviors. Great leaders role model behaviors that are consistent with the values of the organization. Whether it's the CEO or the vice president of sales or a frontline supervisor out in the plant, great leaders walk the talk, demonstrating great leadership behaviors better than average leaders. I believe that leaders should demonstrate certain behaviors inside your organization every day. And I've created a list of those behaviors. You may think of additional behaviors, but these represent the core 22 that I have observed in great leaders across America. The following list precisely describes the kind of behaviors great leaders should exhibit every day to have a positive impact on individuals, teams, and your company's performance. A lot of what separates great leaders from average ones has to do, in part, with how they spend their work day and the consistency they demonstrate. It should be no surprise that average leaders skip a number of these behaviors, or role model them inconsistently or in a poor manner. Good or bad, every behavior has an impact.

Observable Leadership Behaviors

1. Exhibits discipline in how they spend their time
2. Shows appreciation
3. Role models the values of the organization
4. Cares about each individual as a person
5. Talks about the direction in which the organization is going
6. Builds relationships
7. Is flexible when appropriate
8. Exemplifies trust and integrity
9. Does quality work
10. Is action/results oriented
11. Develops others
12. Practices process improvement
13. Is a continual learner (self-development)
14. Holds people accountable with coaching and feedback
15. Shows courage in making tough decisions
16. Makes work simple
17. Is energetic and inspires others
18. Is a strong collaborator
19. Deals with poor performers
20. Delegates responsibility
21. Removes barriers
22. Admits mistakes

These are the kinds of behaviors few leaders demonstrate consistently. Are your current leadership development activities producing managers who are leading by the example you'd prefer? Exceptional leaders understand the importance of personal engagement. They want you to grow. They arrange for your training and development. They offer you special assignments to broaden your workplace and marketplace experiences. They are collaborative. They don't tolerate poor performers. They hold people accountable.

Another quality great leaders demonstrate better than average leaders is showing appreciation. They let their associates take credit for projects while downplaying their own role. They make sure others' efforts are recognized. In a public meeting, they might say, "I really appreciated how you stayed late last Friday to take care of that customer's issue. I just want you to know, on behalf of the entire team, we really appreciate you doing that, because nobody asked you to do it."

There are lots of ways to show appreciation. You can take somebody out to lunch. You can bring in a box of doughnuts. So many managers get too busy with their daily grind to remember to show appreciation. But in reality, it doesn't take much time to do this. The greatest leader I ever worked for gave me a handwritten card every year on my birthday. You can just imagine how that made me feel. This leader cared about my training and development, wanted me to grow, and gave me special assignments so I'd have opportunities to get other experiences in the business. This person was very collaborative and included me in on things.

None of us demonstrates these behaviors as much as we need to. We all can use some growth and development to acquire or improve the "brand" we're presenting. But if you're going to assemble individual development plans, which we will talk about in an upcoming chapter on leadership development, you need such a list to provide feedback. You need to recognize and see these observable behaviors displayed from the CEO on down through the organization, meaning anyone in a leadership position. Whether it's in marketing or in sales, or in operations or in finance or in manufacturing, every part of your business is only as good as its leadership. There is no part of your business that is not impacted by the quality of the leadership running that division or business unit of your company.

Leaders rarely receive effective feedback, unless you leverage a well-designed Leadership 360 process. This process will provide any leader with confidential feedback on their behaviors from their manager, peers, and direct reports. Selecting the observers whose input is most meaningful is a critical upfront part of the process. And the feedback and coaching that follows can be powerful, if discussed and planned with an executive coach.

CHAPTER 5

How to Build a Sustainable Blueprint for Greatness

If you have the right people on the bus, the problem of how to motivate and manage people largely goes away. The right people don't need to be tightly managed or fired up; they will be self-motivated by the inner drive to produce the best results and to be part of creating something great.

—Jim Collins, *Good to Great*

How do you build a sustainable culture? The one-word answer: blueprint. The word insinuates an outline, a framework, a methodology, or a process to build or construct something. In this book, I'm sharing with you one methodology, one process for how to plan more effectively, communicate, and engage your workforce.

The 11 components of my Culture Change Blueprint are based on my 30 years of doing this work as the foundation formula for culture change. This is the formula I have studied and learned and participated in with companies that are extraordinarily successful—the "best of the best." My Culture Change Blueprint is a composite of what 30 great American companies across the United States are following to outperform their competition. They have built enduring, sustainable cultures that outperform, outproduce, and are more profitable than their competitors. This is how they do it, with some small deviation here and there. I could easily have outlined a 30-step process, but I settled on 11 primary components. At a 30,000-foot-level view, this is a more workable framework as you begin to think about how you could launch a culture change initiative in your company.

Can you implement just some steps in this formula? Of course, but you won't have the same impact. If you use the analogy of cooking, this is an 11-step recipe for making lasagna. You may skip a step, but there are some steps you really shouldn't skip, and some that need to occur in a certain sequence.

After citing leadership as the most important driver of a performance culture, respondents agree that communication, alignment with organizational values, employee engagement, and accountability are the next most important components.
—Katherine Ratkiewicz and Ted Garnett, Human Capital Institute Research & PS Culture Matters Webcast, 2013

The Culture Change Blueprint

Here are 11 primary components for building a sustainable culture:

1. Make leadership development a priority

Your executive team must make the decision to design your master plan for developing all three levels of your management team. Before drafting your master plan for developing leaders, I strongly encourage you to take a road trip to visit other successful companies. If three to four members of your executive team take a one-day trip, perhaps two or three different times to different locations, I can assure you that you will approach your planning for leadership development differently. Once you have visited a company that excels in developing leaders, you will come back to your company with a significant shift in your thinking.

A word of caution: Making succession planning a strategic business priority, with the intent of developing the next generation of leaders, is equally critical. One of your measures of success is going to be dependent upon how much of your budget you allocate to making leadership development a business priority, for not only your current but future leaders.

2. **Draft your Human Resource Master Plan**

   I'd like to introduce what I'll refer to as the "5 percent challenge." If your executive team would commit to a disciplined schedule of meetings totaling about 5 percent of each executive's time per month, you could improve your company's customer loyalty, increase morale, reduce errors, double your communication effectiveness, boost revenues, and improve cash flow. Isn't all that worth the 5 percent time commitment? I challenge you to try it for 12 months.

   If you're rolling your eyes at this point, I wouldn't blame you. But here is how the math works. You and your executive team need to be willing to start the year with a very effective, two-day strategic planning session off-site (8 hours x 2 days = 16 hours of strategic planning). A key component is drafting or updating your Human Resource Master Plan after the two-day quarterly planning session. Follow that with three quarterly, eight-hour, off-site sessions to review the previous quarter's priorities, while also validating your upcoming 90-day plan (3 quarters x 8 hours = 24 hours of planning time). Add to that a half-day review session once a month, except January (4 hours x 8 months = 32; it's only eight months because you do not meet for a half day in January or in the three months when you meet for a full day). Now add in one hour a week for an executive review meeting (1 hour x 52 weeks). So, we have 16 + 24 + 32 + 52, for a total of 124 hours annually.

   On the surface, I realize that seems like a lot of time to keep executives away from their desks. But I'm going to institute one more discipline: a seven-minute daily huddle that all executives participate in with every associate in the company at the start of every shift.

Far too many executives and/or business owners do a poor job of planning, not to mention communicating the operational components to others. I am proposing a system that elicits a knee-jerk response from most executives. If you're thinking *I could never sell that at my company because it takes too much time!* you're not alone. Remember, I acknowledged that people have an emotion-based relationship with time. You're only human! But let's invoke your rational side with a bit more math. This will just take a moment.

Assume you are a business owner or executive who works 10.5 hours a day, five days a week. I doubt that, but for argument's sake, let's allot 52.5 for your regular week. Now let's assume you take three weeks of vacation, so multiply 52.5 hours by 49 weeks. You would thus work 2,572 hours a year. The 136 hours of planning time we tallied earlier, plus the seven-minute daily huddle, amount to a whopping 148 hours a year! Well, it seems like a whopper until you do the final math and discover that represents just 5.7 percent of the total 2,572 hours worked.

I've probably made this seem simple, and it is! However, it's not easy, though it is powerful. In less than 6 percent of each executive's time at work, this disciplined sequence of meetings can and will reinvent how your company plans and executes. If every employee, from the C suite to the front line, is on the same page and participating in your seven-minute huddles, morale and engagement have nowhere to go but up.

The daily huddles would be the easiest to "let slide," especially during perceived busy times. But you and your management team must transcend that emotional reaction to the time involved. The huddles are powerful and serve to provide continuity and accountability. They instill a consistent ethic into your organization that will carry through the planning established at the more intensive sessions that take place throughout the year.

Just imagine how alignment, communication, and accountability will improve with this much attention to a disciplined regimen of meetings. Personal accountability increases when every employee shares in their huddle the most important task they must complete that day. It takes time and discipline to get 1,000 associates to make this tempo a priority and actually look forward to these meetings. We achieved this very result in a four-hospital system while surgeries took place and ER visits were underway. Three years later, nurse turnover was reduced to a point that it saved more than $4 million. The daily huddles' quick-tempo agendas improved communication so much that "trust in management" also increased by 89 percent over a two-year period.

You may be thinking it will take your organization a few weeks or months to develop this discipline and get it right. A reporter recently asked a member of the University of Connecticut women's basketball team if Coach Geno Auriemma works everyone hard until they get it right. She answered, "No, we practice it until we can no longer do it wrong." Take a cue from this coach, whose teams have earned ten National Titles, four perfect undefeated seasons, and 22 straight final four appearances. Are you willing to stick to it until you cannot do it wrong?

Speaking of coaching, I have never seen this 5 percent system work without some outside expert training and assistance. And it's worth the investment. It can reinvent how excited your employees are when the culture of your company is engaging and makes it a great place to work. That excitement influences every aspect of how they deliver your product or service. The size of your company doesn't matter. The number of locations in the number of states or countries is not a factor, either. What counts is your executive commitment to a new methodology for planning, communication, execution, and sustainable profitability.

3. Use scaffolding

Three of the best research books you can read are Jim Collins' *Good to Great* and *How the Mighty Fall,* plus Keith McFarland's *The Breakthrough Company.* These books point out that CEOs of companies that substantially outperformed their competition used outside experts better and more strategically than their competition. Leveraging outside experts is no different than bringing in a mergers and acquisition expert to help your company acquire other companies. It is also probable that some executive coaches or consultants can help you locate some best in class companies to visit and benchmark.

Top athletes and singers have coaches. A coach or certified business advisor helps you make the most of your talents, set and achieve performance goals, and claim your place at the top of your game. Once you've reached a major measure of success, you need a coach even more, not less. Top performers are never satisfied with a plateau. IBM retains more than 60 certified coaches on staff. They understand an organization will never outperform its leadership talent. That's why, in a recent survey by Right Management, 86 percent of companies said they use coaching to sharpen the leadership skills of individuals who have been identified as future leaders.

Most executives suffer from limited or filtered feedback, and the higher they get promoted, the less frequent and accurate data they receive. A 2009 *Harvard Business Review* article found 26 percent of executives surveyed hire coaches primarily as a sounding board. Outside objectivity and past executive-level experience are critically important to any senior leader who spends a significant amount of their day attempting to influence others, achieve budget goals, and affect organizational change.

When making a decision to work with a certified executive coach that is so valuable to your career success, look for a coaching firm that offers a system, experience in developing talent, a track record of executive success, referrals, and a great fit for your personality. I often hear executives say it's lonely at the top. Having an executive who is a confidential sounding board will often prove to be invaluable.

4. **Launch your Culture Steering Committee**
Selecting the five to seven associates and/or leaders who are pas-

sionate about change and culture may be one of the most important steps in launching your culture change movement. You only want a mix of senior, middle management, and frontline associates who are wildly excited about the vision of your company. And it can be very powerful to incorporate one or two very trusted frontline employees. Their voice and their communication within the frontline ranks of staff will go a long way toward rolling out the initiatives that will follow.

It's also important that you select participants for the steering committee that have the willingness and courage to lead the change that will be required. The primary responsibilities of the Culture Steering Committee are to research, plan, communicate, and be the positive voice in communicating with company employees as the organization continually improves. I would also encourage you to have your Culture Steering Committee only report directly to your CEO, the CEO must be its sponsor.

5. **Launch your leadership development system**
Once your master plan for developing talent is drafted, you must create an effective baseline of current and past performance for your entire management team. Developing leaders is about performance improvement and developing capability. But first you must answer these questions: Is your management team fit to execute? Do you have the right leaders in the right positions for today and for the near future? The answers to those questions become an important component in whether you are developing the right managers. Who is a great fit for their managerial tasks and responsibilities? Who is or could be a very strong leader? The performance data from each manager's past will serve you well as you begin to develop your leadership scorecard. Start with a comprehensive leadership assessment.

6. **Design a leadership performance scorecard**
More than 90 percent of companies I visit do not have black and

white performance expectations. The output of that lack of clarity is that your company's overall performance will largely be dependent on luck, not design. The power of the scorecard is the holistic view of the 10 metrics it provides. In a healthcare organization with almost 10,000 employees, we could measure and monitor leadership performance on a one-page scorecard.

Developing a scorecard is simple (see Chapter 7). The challenge in the first year is getting senior leaders to use the performance data as a coaching tool. Each manager and/or supervisor or executive must understand that all of the company's efforts toward their development are intended to help leaders perform at a higher level. While the scorecard serves as a great feedback tool, the question that emerges has to do with each senior leader's willingness to tolerate so-so performance, or "C" performers. Ultimately, a scorecard communicates what is acceptable and what is not acceptable performance within an organization, so there is no misunderstanding.

7. **Assess your nine talent management systems**
    Our 30-year track record of designing high-performing cultures revolves around assessing and continuously improving nine specific systems that impact talent, which you can see in Figure 5.

The nine systems addressed are:

☐ **Recruiting**
    What is the gap between your current recruiting system and an industry leader's recruiting system? The quality and quantity of possible candidates will, over time, change the culture of your company and consistently improve your customers' experiences with your business.

☐ **Hiring and selection**
    What changes would your company experience if you hired only "A" or "B" performers for the next five years? Most executives have an inconsistent hiring system that is used by un-

Figure 5

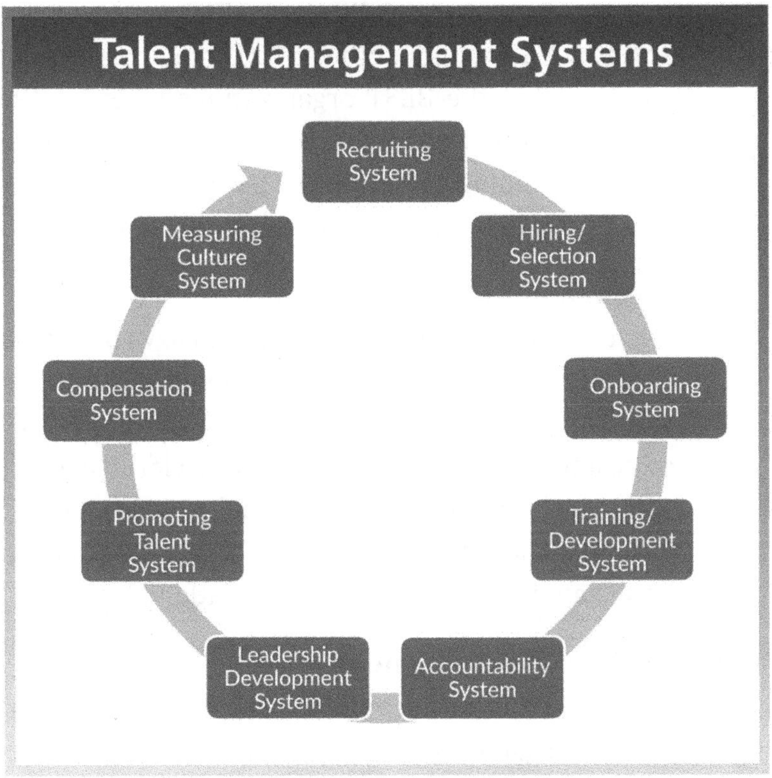

Talent Management Systems

trained professionals, with improper assessment tools. Redesigning your current system will produce better results.

☐ **Onboarding**

What would you save in hard dollars annually if the productivity of all new hires increased significantly, and in a more timely manner, because of how quickly and effectively new associates are oriented at all levels? The onboarding system in great companies can last as much as six months, starting a week prior to their first day at work and continuing on for at least another three months.

☐ **Training and development**

What would it mean to your company profitability and customer loyalty to have the most talented and skilled workforce—only top performers? The amount of time allocated for training makes the difference. The American Society for Training & Development's (ASTD) annual survey shows that employees at the BEST organizations received 49.1 hours of training on average. If your organization offers about 30 hours of training per employee per year, and spends around $1,182 per employee, *you are about average*.

☐ **Accountability**

What would it mean to your culture to have only positive employees who know exactly what their contributions are to your company goals? Training all managers and associates is critical to ensure that employees have clarity about their position, will be held accountable, and will also have their performance measured. In addition, this process also provides important information for compensation planning.

☐ **Leadership development**

What would it be worth to your company over the next two years to significantly increase your leadership talent? Too many companies simply offer training, with very little effort given to conducting a needs assessment by identifying key leadership competencies required in their business. If leaders create the culture of your business through their behaviors, why do so many executives view the budget to develop their management team as such a big expense?

☐ **Promoting talent**

What would it mean to the quality of your management team if only the most talented people were promoted into management positions? How do you currently promote directors, middle managers, associates, or frontline managers? This system should identify and prepare top candidates for promotional options on all levels. Promoting talent is about preparation, planning, and proactive development.

☐ **Compensation**

What would it save you in hard dollars annually if top performers were paid more than average performers and your bonus system was directly tied to the individual's and company's measurable performance? Your company must have a system and every manager must be trained to consistently use the system the way it is intended.

☐ **Measuring culture**

What would it do to your annual profits if you raised your prices, significantly increased your customers' experiences, and tripled your referrals? Your customers' experiences are a reflection of your culture. How can you ever expect to improve your culture if you don't measure it, or if you're unaware of where the problems are?

The intent of this approach is to design and implement these nine systems to attract and retain only top talent and to create an organization that is consistently delivering on its promise to your customers.

Just to give you one example, recently I was at a Vistage CEO event and the speaker, Hunter Lott, referenced that Google hires employees based on adaptability and willingness to learn. Is willingness to learn critical for your new hires?

Promoting the right talent into each leadership position is one of the key nine talent systems. In the 2015 *Gallup State of the American Manager* study, it was found that employees are often placed in managerial roles for reasons that have nothing to do with their *talent to manage*. The top two reasons people become managers are:

1. "I was promoted because I was successful in a previous non-managerial role."

2. "I have a lot of experience and tenure in my company or field."

How would your business be different if you reinvented and prepared the people being promoted into leadership positions within your company?

Designing and/or improving your current nine-talent systems is only half the equation. Once designed, the opportunity then transitions to ensuring that every manager at every level follows and administers the systems and implements each in the way it was designed. Strategic communications, training, and accountability are often critical to the execution and long-term sustainability of each system. Caution: Do not assume; I strongly encourage you to complete a comprehensive assessment of each of the nine talent management systems.

8. Redesign your accountability system

According to a June 21, 1999 article in *Fortune* by Ram Charan and Geoffrey Colvin, failure to execute is still the number one reason for CEO terminations in America today. Execution starts with alignment, as alignment is the result of getting everyone on the same page. Your accountability system is the single most important system you have to align the talent within your company.

Just imagine having a system that permanently eliminates underground resistors from your company. That's right, a company with no more poor performers and/or no one who resists the changes that need to be made. (Even though they may have been in your company for many years, they must go.) Another benefit to an effective accountability system is that it allows you to track individual and/or team performance.

My three-part accountability system differentiates performance from contributions, while clearly pointing out who is not performing up to expectations. This system serves as a great tool for coaching and feedback, not to mention it provides a format for ongoing developmental conversations in a systematic manner. Using such a fair and accurate system for monitoring both individual and team performance will also help you retain top talent, make it easier to promote talent and distribute bonus dollars, and significantly contribute to the leadership scorecard of your entire management team.

9. **Insist on individual development plans (IDPs)**

Are leaders made or are they born to lead? The answer is yes and yes. Some leaders are born with more interpersonal skills. Others can be taught and developed to lead. However, people who naturally possess some leadership traits or competencies are potentially easier to develop into superstar leaders. So when the task at hand is to develop someone, or a team of leaders, it's very possible to develop people already in leadership positions.

Managing and developing executives at three Fortune 500 executive education centers, I have determined that there are two barriers that can prevent any leader, or for that matter anyone, from ever advancing and achieving the personal growth they seek: ego and attitude (as in "I know it all, and I am not willing to be coached/developed"). Yet what would it mean for the effectiveness of your entire management team's leadership competency if every leader annually executed their individual development plan?

Our three-part accountability system requires each leader to codesign and implement their individual development plan. In great organizations, continuous learning and development are not optional. In fact, some organizations make continuous learning a condition of employment.

10. **Assess your current culture**

What if your culture became a real strategic advantage? What if your culture became the primary reason for your revenue growth? So why don't you measure what employees think about working for your company?

Long ago, Peter Drucker stated, "Because the purpose of business is to create a customer, the business enterprise has two—and only two—basic functions: marketing and innovation." Marketing and innovation produce results; all the rest are costs. Marketing is a direct reflection of your organization's culture. Culture represents the preconditions needed for those two basic business functions. You'll notice the words "culture" and "cultivation" are closely related. Anyone who wants to grow anything, whether it's a field of wheat or a successful corporation, first has to have all the elements in place that are conducive to that growth.

Lou Gerstner, former chairman and CEO of IBM said, "Culture isn't just one aspect of the game, it is the game." The Ritz Carlton, Southwest Airlines, and Zappos are often used as shining examples of corporate culture. They're considered great places to work and they consistently outperform their direct competition financially year after year. How can you position your company so it rounds out this list? You must transition your existing culture into a marketing machine that produces a customer experience that differentiates your company and makes people tell others about their experience with you.

According to Gary Tucker, from J.D. Power and Associates, as quoted in the book *The Customer Experience Revolution* by Jeofrey Bean and Sean Van Tyne, "Customer experience is a sustainable advantage. If you can build a model around service, hire and train the right people to deliver the right experience, we know from the data that people will pay for it." Creating that experience begins with the right leaders. Tucker adds that "the top 10 customer experience leaders generated cumulative total returns that were 41 percent better than the S&P 500 Index." Now can there be any doubt about why you should measure your culture?

11. Launch your company university

If recruiting and retaining top talent is to remain a priority for years, I suggest you seriously consider putting a structure in place to train and develop talent at every level in your company. If you decide to organize your talent and develop it into a company university model, make sure you fund it appropriately and have the right person running it. That person must have an extensive learning and development background.

Training is one effective method of spanning the entire management pyramid, from the line supervisor to the C-level, and potentially developing a leadership team consisting only of top producers. Every leader should have an individual development plan (IDP), be focused on their specific development, and/or have the aid of an executive coach. The tools needed to achieve this objective are cutting-edge and include some concepts that you may or may not have heard of, such as neurolinguistic programming (NLP) and emotional intelligence (EQ).

The last two of the five culture metrics that have the biggest effect on financial gains are professional growth and development and alignment with organizational values. This suggests that employees are better positioned to give more discretionary effort when their skills and abilities are being adequately developed and they feel like their organization is actively invested in their success.

—Katherine Ratkiewicz and Ted Garnett,
Human Capital Institute Research &
PS Culture Matters Webcast, 2013

The Right Systems, Processes, and People

After reading through the 11 steps, you may be asking yourself, "Is this really worth it?" One of the business reasons for launching this Culture Change Blueprint is that some of these top-performing companies and cultures in America have created a culture where employees love to work. They treat their customers exceptionally when they call in, deliver their products or service, or handle transactions. What if your business culture was so extraordinary it became a significant marketing strategy to attract more business, because customers wouldn't be able to stop telling people about you? I'm suggesting that your culture and the way you treat employees could create a culture of people who are exceptional and deliver an exceptional customer experience every day.

The Culture Change Blueprint is a formula for taking your company from where it is today to where you'd like it to be by helping you improve your leadership, processes, and people. That's how you execute at a high level. That's what the best cultures in America do really well. Anytime you conduct an assessment of any kind, you are going to get information about your culture and whether you have the right systems and processes in place in your business. That will point to where your company strategy needs to change.

Most privately owned companies do not have a road map, a strategic direction for how to improve their culture. Even if they want to improve, how they go about it oftentimes wastes time, money, and resources. I am a strong proponent that as part of getting started, you visit two or three companies, perhaps outside of your industry, that are four or five years ahead of you on this journey. That means benchmarking. The problem is that most executives have never done benchmarking. They don't really understand what to do, and why they should do it. Benchmarking is nothing more than a strategy for how to continuously improve.

Why wouldn't you take half a day and go study some extraordinary company and learn what they took five years to develop? To me, that seems like an enormous shortcut. When you benchmark, you're there to study the process, not the product they make. You could go to the Harley Davidson plant or a chocolate factory and learn something about quality, systems, processes, leadership, and talent. We were building a cement manufacturing plant and we went to a French fry factory and had an incredible learning experience in a three-hour visit.

If you see the value in benchmarking an organization, I've created a guide for you on how to do that. You can download it free from my website (www.PremierExecutiveForums.com) and it will give you many specific sample questions you should ask when you benchmark.

It is critical for companies to go outside their industry to benchmark the best experience companies.

—Gary Tucker, J.D. Powers & Associates

Yet in order to create the kind of culture that we're describing in this book—a high-performing, highly profitable American company—you're going to need an extraordinarily effective leadership team, including top and middle management, as well as frontline supervisors and team leaders. And that takes us back to the question: "Do I have the right leaders in the right places right now?"

If you're going to make leadership development a priority, and you should, you have to be willing to put forth the resources required to assess and develop your current leadership team. Earlier in the book I referenced "A," "B," and "C" performers. If 20 to 50 percent of your overall leadership team are average performers, you cannot become a best in class company. If you're going to plan for a return on investment, then you're going to have to rethink how you allocate dollars, time, and resources to really develop an extraordinary leadership team on all three levels.

Are the results I have accomplished working inside of companies the kind of results you would like in your organization, whether it's a healthcare system, a manufacturing facility, a dry cleaning operation, or a law practice? It doesn't matter whether you're part of a mid-size or large company. These are the blueprint elements I've always used, and this is one blueprint I recommend you adopt.

CHAPTER 6

Creating Your Own
Leadership Development System

You can double and even triple effectiveness and productivity by exercising individual strengths, talents, and passions.
—Don Clifton, PhD, Selection Research International, 40 years of data on more than 400,000 American men and women

---

Effectively developing leaders requires a system. It's a series of steps. When you study what the best of the best organizations are doing, you ask what kind of methodology do Fortune 100 companies use across America? What kind of methodology does the Center for Creative Leadership use, or Harvard, or and the University of Michigan Business School? They're always number one and number two as top executive education programs in the world.

This chapter is all about launching your own leadership development system. The premise I set out to prove at the beginning of this book is that every company that wants to reach the high-performance level should make leadership development a priority. For those of you who are starting to agree with me and are willing to invest in developing your current and future leaders, you may be asking what would that process look like? How would I do that? I have created an outline you can follow that shows you how to go about it. You'll find it in Figure 6 on the next two pages.

Figure 6

The 12-Step Leadership Development System

COLLECT PAST PERFORMANCE DATA

Step 1: Decide to assess and develop existing leaders

All managers and executives who supervise people in management complete a job analysis survey, plus collect a job description for each position

Step 2: Human Resources assembles 2-3 KPI sources for each manager's past performance data

ASSESS CAPABILITY AND FIT

Step 3: All management completes the leadership assessment

DESIGN THE IDEAL JOB PATTERNS

Step 4: Create a Performance Profile with acceptable ranges for every position in management

Step 5: The director of each position approves the Performance Model drafted in Step 4

PROVIDE MANAGER/EXECUTIVE 1-1 FEEDBACK

Step 6: Conduct a debrief with each manager regarding their assessment "report"

Step 7: Develop an IDP designed for every manager
For example, the IDP may include new assignments, specific projects, etc.

Step 8: Facilitate an executive team debrief for all assessments
Decision time: perhaps select, individual managers may need to be moved into a different role and/or removed from the organization

DEVELOPMENTAL TRAINING AND COACHING IS LAUNCHED

Step 9: Launch leadership training for the entire management team

Step 10: Conduct a Leadership 360 Assessment
Leaders need constructive, honest feedback about their behavior

Step 11: Launch developmental executive coaching related to an individual's IDP

MEASURE PERFORMANCE IMPROVEMENT

Step 12: Measure and monitor performance improvements on leadership scorecard

The 12-step methodology shown in Figure 6 illustrates how many of the best companies develop leaders strategically. I'm sharing with you how the most productive, most profitable companies in America do it. This is my model that I've developed in conjunction with my work. Let's briefly run through each of the steps.

The 12-step process outlined should become an annual process, with some select modification in the first five steps. Each new calendar year a new IDP should be designed and discussed for every manager in your organization for the coming year.

STEP 1

You need some way to link the performance of individuals and leaders to their development. If you're going to put together a leadership development process, you first need to collect some performance data, before you get into the assessment process.

Let me give you an example. Say I had a company with 100 leaders in it—managers, vice presidents, different levels, and I put together a spreadsheet that would pull together this information. I'd be looking for data about the customer feedback from each of those departments. What was each manager's performance review like for the last three years? What's turnover or employee retention in their department been like for the last three years? What have customer satisfaction scores been like for each leader's area of responsibility? What kind of quality of work is coming out of those departments? I could go on. So collecting some past performance data is part of Step 1. Once I do that, I can complete a job analysis for each position. I also want to collect job descriptions, a definition of responsibilities for each of those 100 positions.

Most organizations, at this point, realize they don't even have job descriptions written down, or something that defines the skills, capabilities, and responsibilities of a position. Just doing that, putting together that data in and of itself, is progress. So there's no real assessment in Step 1. It's about starting with and understanding the information you already have. This data will also serve as a baseline for future measurement and performance improvement.

STEP 2

How are you going to monitor and measure the performance of leaders across the system and across the organization? In Step 2 you start to zero in and create a methodology to track progress. You begin to figure out the key performance indicators (sometimes called KPI). You need to assemble as much key performance information as you can, and in Step 2 you begin to organize it into something that could be considered a scorecard.

STEP 3

In Step 3 you conduct an assessment. Different assessments are used in different companies for different reasons. While there are a few thousand leadership assessment tools available, we believe we have access to some of the greatest leadership assessment tools on earth. We use the correct assessment tool that's statistically valid and would even stand up in court. You would ask everybody in management to complete the assessment, which will range in time anywhere from 30 minutes to an hour and a half, depending on the complexity of the assessment and which assessment is actually selected.

STEP 4

Once you've collected the information, in Step 4 you begin to create a description for each position in management. This is a profile of what a great, high-performing manager, vice president or team leader would look like in this position. When you take the assessment data and compare it to the profile, you're going to start learning about where your company may have performance opportunities for improvement.

STEP 5

In Step 5, you draft a model of a talented, high-performing person for each position. In other words, what would a profile of a "great" person in this position look like? What kinds of skills and capabilities and behaviors would this person need, as an ideal?

Once you make that determination, you need to validate the performance ranges in each of those areas. For example, if one of the skills and competencies of a high-performing manger is communication, what level of that skill is required, using a scale of 1 to 10? In this position, the range of skill required may be from 7 to 9 in terms of importance, frequency, and how valuable that skill might be. In another position that's more of a research position, communication skills might only need to be in a range of 4 to 7, because it's more analytical on a scale of 1 to 10.

Different positions can require different capabilities. Some positions may require a lot of skill in strategic thinking, working with practical information, collaboration, risk taking, independent thinking, and entrepreneurial kinds of spirited behavior and activities. Other positions may require the opposite, people who are extraordinarily process and systems driven.

STEP 6

In Step 6, each person who has completed the assessment in Step 3 receives feedback about their assessment. I should point out that the assessment in Step 3 is not a test; you don't pass or fail. Here is where you'll learn the true demands of the job and the requirements. And the assessment report is going to show you some of the strengths of that manager, areas of developmental needs, and possibly that you don't have the right person in the job.

Then, each person receives an executive debrief about how they did on that assessment. The debrief can occur in a couple of ways. As a certified executive coach, sometimes I am asked to conduct the debriefs. Sometimes we'll have a debrief training session, where we'll get groups of people together to explain the report before they're given to the people who went through the assessment. Sometimes the manager of the person will handle the debrief and I will coach or train the manager on how to do that.

The result is that every single manager in the organization will be aware of one or more specific leadership skills, areas, or behaviors that they need to improve. You can look at Steps 1 through 6 as a giant needs assessment. Now you'll know where to focus in the development of every single manager in the organization.

STEP 7

In Step 7 you begin to create that individual development plan, or an IDP, for every single manager in the organization. What did you learn, now that you've put all 100 people through the assessments? Do you have the right people in the right positions? Do you have people who are fit to execute? Do you have managers you can develop who are keepers? These would be people you know who can do the job today and in the future.

Development strategies may appear in many different forms or possibilities. To assist you in planning strategies for your or any manager's IDP, here is a list of 23 strategies to expand your thinking of how to expedite someone's development:

1. Classroom leadership training
2. Participation in a leadership development program
3. Completing an eLearning module
4. Mentoring assignments
5. Extra work assignments
6. Reading leadership books
7. Reading journals
8. Cross-training
9. Rotational assignments
10. On-the-job training
11. Executive coaching
12. Interviewing an exemplary performer
13. Special project involvement
14. Shadowing another performer
15. Internships
16. Joining a volunteer board of directors
17. Evening school
18. Benchmarking/visiting other businesses

19. Attending university executive education programs
20. Allowing high potentials to interact with their future manager
21. Designing developmental assignments that may have in-between steps for possible career progression
22. Special problem-solving task force assignments
23. Selecting challenging work assignments

STEP 8

In Step 8 you're going to have that tough conversation with your executive team. You're also probably going to be talking about whether you may have some people who need to move into a different position because they were promoted beyond their competency level. And you'll discuss whether you have the right leaders in the right positions who are willing to be developed. So there are some tough decisions that can occur at this step. It is also possible that select individuals may be asked to leave your organization.

STEP 9

How can you begin to systematically create leadership training and development for your management team? There are a lot of details that can go into that training. When you study some of the best organizations in the world and their skills in communication, delegation, problem-solving, decision-making, etc., there are many effective leaders who seem to use those skills effortlessly. Developing your managers to make that happen is what Step 9 is all about, and it can often be done in a very organized, systematic way.

In Chapter 5 we talked about launching a company university. Creating a company university is one systematic way to offer training and development for people across your organization. A corporate university model will become a very powerful recruiting and retention model as well, especially given the importance millennials place on development.

Consider these three statements of fact about training, from the article "How to Make Staff Training Pay for Itself" by Tom Borg of Tom Borg Consulting:

- ☐ Xerox Corporation reported that for every dollar they spend on training, they get a return of $22.

- ☐ IBM Corporation reported that they received $26 for every dollar they invested on training.

- ☐ Motorola Corporation reported that they get a ROI of $33 for every dollar spent on training.

Now go look at your budget for training your greatest assets.

STEP 10

Step 10 is about giving leaders that all-important feedback. In Step 10 you ask employees for feedback about the behaviors (see Chapter 4 for examples) of their leaders: how they communicate, how they go through their day, how they start meetings. Most of these behaviors are critical in creating a high-performing culture.

One way to get additional developmental feedback is by conducting a 360 Survey. In fact, you can conduct a 360 Survey of your entire leadership team, starting at the top. We'll be covering the 360 Survey in more detail in the next chapter, but for now, I'll just say a 360 Survey is what the name implies: You collect feedback from your manager, your peers, and your direct reports. Oh, and you would include an assessment of yourself for comparison.

Another form of feedback is your culture survey, asking employees what it's like to work at the company. When you conduct a culture survey, you're going to get feedback about what it's like to work for a particular manager. If a manager scores low on the culture survey three years in a row, that would be part of the performance data that you collected in Steps 1 and 2.

This feedback is part of helping leaders grow, develop, and continuously improve. Step 10 gives you additional information for creating an IDP for each and every manager and helps you determine in which areas you should focus that development.

STEP 11

In Step 11 you begin to launch executive coaching as a way to develop individuals. You can use outside executive coaches. You can bring in a team of outside experts. You can also do an extraordinary amount of development in your own organization by developing a culture of coaching and having three to ten managers and leaders who become certified as internal executive coaches.

There are lots of examples of companies that use both models. Just keep in mind that most leaders would benefit from having a private coaching session with an outside expert. There are frequently issues that an executive simply is not willing to share or discuss with anyone inside the organization.

Most executives suffer from limited or filtered feedback, and the higher they are promoted, the less frequent and accurate data they receive. The 2009 *Harvard Business Review* article "What Can Coaches Do for You?" found 26 percent of executives surveyed hire coaches primarily as a sounding board. Outside objectivity and past executive-level experience are critically important to any senior leader who spends a significant amount of their day attempting to influence others, achieve budget goals, and affect organizational change.

In early 2012, the nation's largest study of executive coaches, by Sherpa Coaching, revealed that "the majority of executive coaching is designed for leadership development," and it achieves it in these five primary ways:

1. Allows a leader to reflect on and learn from decisions
2. Exposes a leadership behavior that may be limiting effectiveness
3. Leads personal career development
4. Strategically leads organizational change
5. Provides a sounding board

When confidentiality and performance improvement are critical, internal mentoring can only go so far. And having a strategic advisor can pay for itself many times over, since the impact of one strategic decision may reap millions of dollars in value over the next one to three years. Obviously, the fit between an executive and a coach is invaluable in establishing the trust essential for achieving optimal performance. Experience is critically important when selecting a team of outside experts to coach key members of your leadership team. A coach with a proven track record can help transform cultures one executive at a time.

The majority of coaching is facilitated via phone, live, or by use of webcam. More than 90 percent of all executive coaching relationships start with one or two assessments that reveal the leader's strengths and development needs. Think of it as a powerful diagnostic tool, a kind of leadership MRI, if you will. Great assessments, in combination with excellent interpretation skills, enable executive coaches to know the leader from the inside out. A coach for each key executive will help strategically make every employee's unit a great place to work.

In the last 10 years, a team approach has arrived on the scene, adding a new dimension in executive coaching. The concept is similar to that of individual coaching, but caters to the many egos, strengths, and styles present in a department or group. Often, differing communication styles could represent one possible dynamic that prevents organizational alignment and success within a team.

Whatever the details of the arrangement, it is critical that parameters be set upfront about who is going to receive what feedback. A high level of trust is non-negotiable. Any CEO must know anything he/she shares with the coach will not be shared with anyone. Executive coaching is about helping the executive with all the issues already on his/her plate, and any in the future; it's not about adding to those responsibilities. In fact, delegation is often a stumbling block for leaders. Therefore, conversations about the talents and skill levels of direct reports are common during the coaching process so the executive can delegate more effectively.

In our 2012 national study, 39.6 percent of executives surveyed gave themselves a failing grade in their planned approach to developing their leaders. To make matters worse, 39.6 percent of executives said less than half of their organization executes its plan of top priorities consistently. The right coach can absolutely help leaders execute at a higher level. More than 60 percent of executives that completed the national study scored the value of executive coaching as "very high."

Before making a decision so valuable to your career success, look for a coaching firm that offers experience, a coaching system, past referrals, a track record of executive success and developing talent, and a great fit for your personality. As Dr. Atul Gawande wrote in his article "Top Athletes and Singers Have Coaches. Should You?", "Coaching done well may be the most effective intervention designed for human performance."

In his book *First Break all The Rules*, Marcus Buckingham's research proved that organizations with the highest levels of engagement were more likely to have 56 percent higher customer loyalty. But before even picking up the phone to contact an executive coach, make sure you take a hard look in the mirror and ask yourself: "Am I coachable? Do I know how to systematically create a culture obsessed with customer care, or could I use a little help? Am I consistently measuring engagement in my company? Do I understand how to strategically measure my 'customer experience?' "

STEP 12

This is the final step in a leadership development model. You've got to keep score. You've got to know if you're making a difference. And leaders need to be held accountable.

Step 12 is about measurement, being able to monitor performance. You implemented all 11 steps. Now you have to keep score. Are people improving their leadership capabilities? How do you know? You ask employees. You look at your customer feedback scores. You look at your employee feedback scores. You look at the 360 Survey feedback scores.

Your job is to constantly be feeding information back to leaders about their effectiveness. Without feedback, you don't know if people are growing and developing. You don't know if the coaching is working. You don't know if people are applying the training they're learning. You don't know if people are taking the feedback seriously. If you're going to build a culture of continuous improvement, you have to keep score. In Chapter 7 we'll go over samples of what a leadership scorecard might look like.

Employees at BEST organizations experienced 49.1 hours on average annually [of training] and averaged over 40 hours per employee for the last seven years. So if your organization offers about 30 hours of training per year, and spends around $1,182 per employee, you are about average.

—2012 ASTD Annual Report

What about Your Future Leaders?

My experience would suggest that if you could give every leader in your organization periodic, honest feedback about the observable behaviors that were listed in Chapter 4, your organization would go a long way toward improving the effectiveness of its leadership team. This process I've outlined, the 12-Step Leadership Development System, is a process that does just that. And I'd like to point something out here: Most business owners and/or executives do not place enough importance on their frontline supervisors' development. They manage your associates that serve your customers every day. You must invest an equal amount of money on the training and development of all managers, or more on team leaders and foremen.

At the beginning of every year, each leader in your company should be required to have an IDP. Their plan should be based on one or two competencies or behaviors that leader would like to improve, which could make the difference between an average and exceptional performer. That particular manager and their boss would have a dialogue and put together an IDP to improve that behavior or skill. Then, throughout the year, that leader would receive continuous feedback and each manager would use the IDP as a coaching tool and hold each direct report accountable for the execution of his/her individual de-

velopment plan. As that process just keeps looping, you create an organization where development is a priority. It's funded, and there's a
budget for people in leadership positions to be gaining developmental kinds of experiences.

Development can come in many forms. I've only mentioned a couple here, leadership training and executive coaching. What you need
to understand is that an organization's commitment to developing
leaders has to include a budget for the next 10 years, if you want your
leadership team to be filled with rock stars, people who are the best
of the best, and funding is essential.

Remember, I told you earlier in this book you have only four options for improving your leadership: 1.) You can tolerate the performance of your existing leadership team; 2.) you can work with an
executive search firm and buy new talent (in some cases that's a very
good option, but I don't know if you'd want to do that if you have 40
openings on your leadership team); 3.) you can assess and develop
the leaders you already have; or 4.) simply combine strategies two
and three.

What we've walked through in this chapter is the third option,
a systematic way to strategically develop the current leaders in
your organization at all three levels—frontline supervisors, middle
management department heads and directors, and vice presidents
and above. However, this 12-Step Leadership Development System
will not only improve your team's current performance, it will help
your organization build a pool of talent that has been identified and
systematically developed to provide your company with the next
generation of high-performing leaders, creating meaningful bench
strength. Bench strength will serve you well today, while ensuring
you are developing the next generation of leaders who will someday
be directors and vice presidents.

CHAPTER 7

How Well Are You
Tracking Your Progress?

---

*The inability of CEOs (business owners) to successfully translate
their strategy into execution and results is considered to be the
number one reason why CEOs (business owners) fail.*

—Ram Charan and Geoffrey Colvin, *Fortune*

Whether you call it an accountability system or a performance management system, it's still a system to measure and track progress. You need some way to keep score. You need to know whether your leadership development program is effective in improving your company's culture and other key indicators.

Execution starts with alignment, or what some people call "getting everybody on the same page." How can you possibly execute at a high-level consistently if you don't have everybody on the same page? There is power in alignment. The greater your alignment, the higher your probability will be of hitting your organizational priorities, which means profits, customer loyalty, and strategic growth.

Most leaders have a very skewed perception of alignment in their organization. If you think your organization's done a pretty good job of this, I would encourage you as a CEO to go for a walk in your business and find some frontline employees, some managers, some everyday associates that do a good job, and ask them to honestly answer one question: "Can you tell me, Mr./Ms. Employee, what are the two or three most important responsibilities that you're being held accountable for, regarding this year's performance? You and your manager have discussed them, you agreed to them, and you actually have them in writing somewhere at your desk. If I asked your boss, would he or she state the same two or three specific responsibilities?"

In 98 percent of the organizations I've visited, most employees cannot answer that question with specifics. They don't know how what they do contributes to the organization's success. Their manager has not talked about the priorities of the organization as those priorities relate to their job. Unfortunately, a very large percentage of middle managers and frontline managers will also fail the same question. Now are you still wondering why your company is not growing to become an industry leader?

Just to be clear, I am describing priorities far superior to how most leaders think. The best companies, as studied by Keith McFarland in his *The Breakthrough Company* research, "tended to be ruthless at determining priorities." What kind of a gap do you have in your company with regards to you becoming ruthless at determining your priorities?

If you have an organization with 1,000 employees, and 9 out of 10 employees can't answer that question, you start to wonder what they do every day. Unfortunately, most of them are busy. It's one of the two four-letter words that prevent organizations from growing. But are they getting the right things done every day? Probably not. If you're not getting everybody on the same page, if you haven't created alignment, how do you expect your company to do a great job of delivering on its organizational goals? Everybody in your organization needs to be focused on the same results. Every employee must be able to see how their contribution of results contributes to the organization's key performance indicators.

Hey, What's the Score?

When you measure the effectiveness of leaders, every manager must know what they're being held accountable for. Let me repeat this . . . When you measure the effectiveness of leaders, every manager must know what they're being held accountable for. That's where it starts, with the management team, and all three levels of management—senior leaders, middle managers, and frontline supervisors. You're in alignment. Your employees, all of them, understand the company's goals and their specific, measurable responsibilities. They know what's expected of them.

Next, you need to track their performance. You need some sort of scorecard. It's like going to a football game and having a scoreboard in the end zones. This chapter is about using organizational tools to help you stay on track, so as a CEO or an executive team, you won't have to guess just how well your business is performing, you'll know. These tools will allow you to effectively monitor and measure performance and then use the data to make adjustments when necessary.

Let's go over an example. The Leadership Performance Scorecard in Figure 7 on the next page was created for a healthcare system, for leadership only. You'll notice that we have created some definitions, 10 ways that we would measure the performance of all management. Then we defined what we considered to be "poor," "mediocre," "good," "very good," and "outstanding" performance. We created three columns—D, E, and F—for each of the criteria where we have a scale.

If an employee's score for one of the measures was under a certain level, it would be in the far right-hand column, labeled F in that category. (By the way, you can find a color version of this scorecard on my website and print it out, if you'd like, at www.PremierExecutiveForums.com; click on "book graphic.")

If their performance for each of the 10 metrics was okay or good or mediocre, meaning they fell in the middle of the range, their score would be in column E. If their score for the criteria was exceptionally high, then it would be a strength, and it would be scored in column D.

Figure 7

Leadership Performance Scorecard

Definition of Criteria

	A	B	C	D	E	F
1	Dimension	Detailed Definition	Data Source	Strength	Proficient	Development Need
2	PA for 2008	Performance Appraisal for 2008 scored in 2008 on a 150-point scale	People Soft/Personnel Files	Score => 120	Score between 100 and 119.99	Score < 100
3	PA for 2007	Performance Appraisal for 2007 scored in 2007 on a 100-point scale	People Soft/Personnel Files	Score => 90	Score between 70 and 89.99	Score < 70
4	Job Satisfaction	December 2008 Associate Survey Job Satisfaction	Employee Opinion Survey Mapping produced by HR Score derived from 2008 Report	Percentage => 80%	Percentage between 62% and 79%	Percentage < 62%
5	Supervisory Consideration	December 2008 Employee Survey Supervisory Effectiveness	Employee Opinion Survey Mapping produced by HR Score derived from 2008	Percentage => 76%	Percentage between 58% and 75%	Percentage < 58%
6	Patient/ Customer Satisfaction	2008 Unit/Patient Satisfaction Score OR CRA Internal Customer Survey Score	Report produced by HR and Operations Analysis	Percentage => 1.5% variance of target	Percentage between 0% and 1.49% variance of target	Percentage < 0% variance of target
7	Budget Performance	Achieved 2008 Budget Performance Targets	Report produced by HR and Finance Administration	Percentage => 1.5% variance of target	Percentage between 0% and 1.49% variance of target	Percentage < 0% variance of target
8	Separation Rate	2008 Department Separation Rate	HR Separation Rate Report	Percentage < 11.9%	Percentage between 11.9% and 14.78%	Percentage => 14.79%
9	Leadership Training	Attended 16 hours of Leadership Training	Grade Point	Attended ALL required training	Attended SOME required training	Did not attend ANY required training
10	Management Training	Attended 4 Lunch and Learn Sessions	Grade Point	Attended ALL required training	Attended SME required training	Did not attend ANY required training

☐ Exceeds Target   ☐ Meets Target   ☐ Below Target

Let's take a closer look at just one of the criteria, number four, labeled "job satisfaction." We used an employee engagement survey with 10 questions to create a score for each manager. If their score cumulatively was below a certain number, they were scored in column F. If their score was pretty good, they would score in column E. If they scored exceptionally, very high for those 10 questions, they would be in column D. That would indicate on that particular leadership score that the employees were engaged, they liked working for their manager, and they enjoyed the feedback they received.

The second scorecard, in Figure 8, adds employee names. Again, across the top of the scorecard are the 10 categories. Then we plug in red, yellow, and green. (If it would be easier for you to read, you can download the scorecard in color from my website at www.PremierExecutiveForums.com; click on "book graphics.")

In our example, you see somebody with the name T. Jackson. Mr. or Ms. Jackson has something like seven out of the 10 categories below target. I'm thinking that Mr./Ms. Jackson's boss might want to have a conversation with Mr./Ms. Jackson, because the scorecard is indicating he/she is not doing a very good job of delivering on the results he/she has been asked to deliver.

Figure 8

NTS Health
2011 Leadership Performance Scorecard

NUMBER	LAST NAME	FIRST NAME	DEPARTMENT NAME	ATTENDED 16 HOURS LEADERSHIP TRAINING 2011	DECEMBER 2011 P/A SCORE > 80	2011 WORKFORCE SURVEY ASSOCIATE ENGAGEMENTS 75%	2011 ASSOCIATE SURVEY SUPERVISORY EFFECTIVENESS > 70%	2011 UNIT/PATIENT SATISFACTION SCORES > 60% OR CRA INTERNAL CUSTOMER SURVEY SCORE > 40%	ACHIEVED 2011 BUDGET PERFORMANCE TARGETS	2011 SURVEY PARTICIPATION RATE > 80%	2011 DEPARTMENT SEPARATION RATES < 15%	DECEMBER 2010 P/A SCORE > 120	ATTENDED 4 SERVICE EXCELLENCE MODULES 2011	TOTAL POINTS
Maximum Points Possible				10	10	10	10	10	10	10	10	10	10	100
1	Donovan	M.	CSB	10	79	93	86	56.1 PG	6	81	9%	125	3	483.09
3	Jordan	P.	Clinical	0	95	96	91	49.1 PG	2	95	15%	140	7	526.15
4	Collier	M.	Bed Control	10	89	66	71	28.9 INTERNL	8	94	16%	122	5	465.16
5	Knop	R.	Care Mgmt	10	84	74	66	49.1 PG	5	72	4%	121	8	440.04
6	Ditmore	J.	Environmental	0	77	53	45	30.4 PG	2	88	11%	143	5	413.11
7	Bora	G.	Facility	10	74	88	94	16.6 INTERNL	9	63	10%	132	6	476.10
8	McPark	K.	Security	0	95	73	70	40.3 INTERNL	6	82	13%	127	9	462.13
9	Jackson	T.	CSB	10	70	65	87	22.5 PG	3	75	19%	110	2	422.10
10	Munsey	R.	Administration	10	78	70	74	40.1 INTERNL	4	82	16%	120	10	448.16
11	Bunce	K.	CSB	10	83	80	82	70.8 INTERNL	9	79	7%	125	9	477.07
12	Wilkie	B.	Administration	10	91	81	70	56.1 PG	7	87	13%	137	7	490.13
13	Foster	K.	Coronary Care	10	85	68	65	61.8 PG	5	96	27%	128	4	461.27
14	Miller	K.	Progressive Care	10	78	82	73	94.6 INTERNL	7	83	14%	95	5	433.14
15	Hutchens	D.	Pediatrics	10	80	64	55	57.0 PG	2	62	15%	97	2	372.15
16	Brogan	N.	Admin-Nursing	10	73	64	63	31.7 INTERNL	1	78	31%	84	10	383.31

Exceeds Target   Meets Target   Below Target

As far as these scorecards go, you can create scorecards by department, by work unit, or by plant. If you have a company that only has a 25-person management team, you could show all 25 managers on a two- or three-page spreadsheet and it would give you an accurate reflection of just how well your team is doing. The scores reflected on the scorecard should be in direct alignment with how the company is performing.

...there's an alarming disconnect between the parts of the organization that formulate corporate strategy and the functions, processes, and people required to execute it.

—Robert S. Kaplan and David P. Norton,
Harvard Business Review

Aligned and Accountable

What are your customer satisfaction scores telling you? What about your employee engagement, culture survey, revenue, profitability, and employee turnover targets? Depending on what your company comes up with for targets and measurable criteria, these scores will give you a pulse on how well your company is meeting those targets, and if immediate adjustments need to be implemented.

There are two main ways to keep score and help your executives coach, provide feedback, monitor and measure performance, and keep everybody aligned to the organization's priorities. One of them is the leadership scorecard. The second system is what we refer to as the performance management system. It's a system used to create alignment. It's a system designed for accountability. It's meant to be an annual 12-month system, whether your company is on a July 1 to June 30 cycle, or a January 1 to December 31 cycle. Figure 8, which we'll discuss in more detail shortly, illustrates this system.

The power in using this system is twofold. First, you can get everybody on the same page. Second, you'll have a system in place to provide coaching and feedback to employees at every level in the organization about how every individual and your teams are perform-ing. What would be different in your business if you built a culture of powerful coaching and feedback?

While most organizations have a performance management sys-tem, employees and managers tend to dislike it. It's often poorly de-signed, poorly used, and managers have never been trained in how to use the system effectively. And I'm going to guess that 95 percent of companies do not use the system they already have because leaders don't hold managers accountable for accountability.

At the end of the year, you're going to sit down with your manager for your review, and it's likely you'll be surprised when your manager brings up situations and/or feedback examples from seven months ago. So the coaching and feedback you're going to get will not be very timely. While employees dread year-end reviews, managers don't like giving year-end reviews, either; and they tend to overinflate them, giving employees better than average feedback. Therefore, even poor performers get an average review. Yet if those year-end reviews were used effectively, if your organization adopted a philosophy and a new passion about how to use this tool to create organizational alignment, and then hold people accountable, it would provide good, honest, fair feedback.

It's a system that gives both individuals and teams the opportu-nity to be able to recognize performance because it focuses on indi-vidual and team accomplishments and talents in a measurable way. It also lets people know what's expected of them, and that what they do matters. It helps facilitate employee feedback and coaching on how to improve performance. And it aids managers in talking about the growth and development of each employee. So, all in all, an effective performance management system helps employees grow and learn. Furthermore, this type of system helps identify who needs some extra attention and some different type of coaching and feedback.

In addition to results and individual development plans, your per-formance management systems should provide feedback for how well every associate demonstrates behaviors that are in alignment with the values of your company. People tend to get hired based on their résumé and past performance, but most people who get terminated are failing to live up to the values of the company. How effectively have you communicated "how" work gets done in your company? If collaboration is a value in your company, how well do people at all levels collaborate?

As a manager, a scorecard really helps you deliver on the key performance goals that you're being held accountable for when you can get your employees accountable and aligned to those priorities. And when you can accurately give people feedback on their individual contributions and how they did compared to what's expected of them, your system will provide end-of-the-year scores that allow you to feed into your compensation planning and accurately link performance to money, whether it's annual increases in base pay, a bonus program, a profit-sharing program, or a gain sharing program.

Organizations don't execute unless the right people, individually and collectively, focus on the right details at the right time.

—Larry Bossidy and Ram Charan,
Execution: The Discipline of Getting Things Done

Feedback and Coaching Make the Difference

If there was one skill above all others that could help make a performance management system work more effectively, it's that leaders become incredibly skilled at coaching and feedback, so they could sit down with individuals, have a performance conversation, and understand how they can help people on their team grow, develop, and perform at a higher level. Yet most people in management have never been trained to be an effective coach.

Your performance management system ought to be tied to the performance of your organization. If you set annual goals and targets, whether they're related to revenue, profitability, customer growth, or market share, it doesn't matter. At the beginning of the year, people ought to know what's expected of them with written, measurable goals. Those goals should be Specific, Measurable, Achievable, Realistic, and Timebound (SMART).

As the illustration in Figure 9 shows, there are three components to the annual 12-month cycle. If you think of it as a clock, the top third, from about 10:00 to 2:00, is the planning component. It suggests that at the beginning of a calendar year, once the goals and direction for the organization are set, the CEO would sit down with his or her direct reports, vice presidents, and set their performance targets for the year. Then those vice presidents and senior leaders would sit down with their middle management, their department heads, their managers, and have the same alignment conversation. Each department head would know their performance targets for the year, and those department heads, in turn, would have the same conversation with their direct reports, the frontline managers, who would have the same conversation with the in-

Figure 9

dividuals on their team. The goal setting process of creating alignment is a top-down driven process when executed correctly.

When you do that effectively, by the end of February every single employee in your organization ought to know, in writing, what's expected of them. It should not be done via an email but a conversation (you'll see the word discussion in the center of the circle). These are facilitating discussions that create alignment.

The second section of the three-part cycle is coaching. You'll notice in Figure 9 there is ongoing coaching and periodic feedback. At the beginning of the year, everybody gets in writing what's expected of them. In the middle of the year, you have a mid-year review discussion. The mid-year review ought to be very easy to document and discuss. During the mid-year and year-end reviews, employees should also take part in self-appraisals. I'm a huge proponent of self-appraisals. (If you'd like to see a sample of what they look like, you can download one from my website at www.PremierExecutiveForums.com).

When we do accountability training inside organizations, we like employees to come to their reviews with some documentation about how they think they've performed—a very simple, one-page document. These are activities that were above and beyond their basic responsibilities. Maybe they volunteered for a project that required some extra attention on a weekend, maybe they worked on a holiday to take care of a customer.

At the end of the year, everybody gets a year-end review. And when you provide 11 months of coaching and feedback, the year-end review ought to be pretty easy, with no surprises. The feedback and coaching, like in sports, in a band, on a debate team, is to help people continually improve. The 11 months in between the beginning and end of the year is where organizations tend to drop the ball. That's when managers ought to be providing an effective culture of coaching and feedback, above other skills. To quote a McKinsey study referenced in a MIT Sloan article, "although formal leadership training plays an important role, by far the most critical tools to improve performance are intensive, individual feedback and coaching."

As a manager, either you have a team filled with all-stars, of which there are very few, or you understand how to coach and provide feedback, and help people continually improve their performance throughout the year. There are two kinds of feedback: You can reinforce or give compliments, and you can redirect, which means somebody is not meeting expectations and needs some different kind of coaching.

If you go back to the scorecard at the beginning of this chapter, the scorecard provides feedback. You build a system to provide feedback so managers know how they're doing. It gives their boss, their manager, a tool to intervene, help improve, and find out what part of the 10 components of performance is causing someone's scores to have so many below target categories.

If you're not going to provide effective coaching and feedback throughout the year, if you're not going to follow the annual cycle the way it's designed, your only other chance of success is to keep your fingers crossed and hope and pray. We always tell people in our performance management training, there's a secret to having year-end reviews that are easy, positive, and both the employee and the manager look forward to them. The secret is that managers at every level hold managers accountable for using the performance management system the way it's designed . . . leaders holding leaders accountable for accountability. In his book *The Five Temptations of a CEO*, Patrick Lincioni is quoted as saying, "Without accountability, results are just a matter of luck."

When you do that in your company, hold leaders accountable, the entire focus of the organization begins to shift, and when that happens, watch your results, watch quality and morale begin to improve. Watch employee engagement and customer loyalty increase. Watch the measures in your company begin to improve when leaders hold leaders accountable. This is about taking an organization with 1,000 employees from being "busy" to being really focused and aligned to the priorities of the organization. When you create that alignment, and you use the performance management system for coaching and feedback, and you measure along the way, you're successfully using your accountability system. Now you have substantially improved your probability that your organization may reach the next level. And if this system isn't being used well in your organization, it's an executive responsibility. Are you looking for the root cause of your lack of growth and execution? The answer is leadership.

CHAPTER 8

It's All about the Customer

Execution requires engaging the hearts and minds of people who have to do the hard work. Only about 40% of people know exactly what to do and only 33% say they are enabled to use all their talent.

—Larry Bossidy and Ram Charan,
Execution: The Discipline of Getting Things Done

The word customer has come up several times in this book. You probably realize there are two different types of customers when it comes to business. One of them is your internal customer. When we talk about leadership and leadership development, we could easily focus on your internal customers, whom we've labeled as associates, employees, or the direct reports of leaders. These are the full-time, part-time, or contract workers who contribute to your daily business success. Your other customer is the external person or the company that buys your product or service.

By now you should be very aware of the concept that the people who surround leaders, and how those leaders are developed, significantly impact the culture of an organization, both internally and externally. Your leaders actually create your company's culture by the way they treat your employees, which impacts how those employees treat your external customers and/or by how they allow your employees to behave. Your employees not only follow company systems and policies and do the work every day to deliver a product or service to your external customers, their work environment influences the manner in which they deliver those products or services.

Your external customers then either become loyal or NOT. They either have a great experience with your company or they have an average experience. If they have a great experience, they return and tell lots of others about your business and the great experience they had and bring you referrals and other potential customers. Ask your management team today, do you simply sell your product or service, or do you sell your product or service and ___? The blank is important. What if your company becomes known for how well it delivers more than people expect (the ___)? I would like to challenge every leader or business owner who reads this book to come up with your company's definition of what a great customer experience would be like for every customer you touch in the next 10 years.

When you look at your company's alignment around skills and competencies, you need to think about how you should be developing your leaders, because they will determine the kind of culture you're ultimately going to have in the next three to five years. And how well you develop those leaders will ultimately help determine if your company is going to become an industry all-star. Here are some questions for CEOs to consider:

- ☐ How does your company's current performance compare to your vision of where you think your business could or should be?

- ☐ How does your company's current performance compare to your industry's leaders?

- ☐ What are you doing systematically to develop your leaders?

- ☐ What percentage of your entire management team would you rehire because they are exceptional performers?

What Makes You Stand Out?

How does leadership development differentiate your company? Why is differentiation so important? In today's economy, most businesses have only three ways to compete: by price, by product, or by service. Playing the price game is dangerous as your company evaluates its margins. And if you're not going to be the cheapest—if you're going to be in the middle of the price pack with your competitors, or one of the more expensive—you need to be different.

I've asked thousands of managers and executives at events across the nation, how would you rate service in your city, across a lot of industries? The answer is always the same: companies simply have become average. People tend to get what they pay for, nothing more. Those responses suggest that in almost every market across America, there's an opportunity that exists for some company, some executive, some CEO, some executive team to stand out and become a service leader in their industry.

There are so many little ways you can be different. For example, there are some companies out there that have made the delivery of their service so simple, so unique, it's differentiating them. Zappos has capitalized on one little principle—return it for free, and we'll make it easy. While there are hundreds of companies you can buy shoes or clothing from online, Zappos, with their free, easy return policy, is becoming an industry leader. It's not because they're the cheapest. There's a business reason for that differentiation. Southwest Airlines is trying to make flying a "fun" experience. Southwest Airlines was built on a principle of making flying a fun experience because flying is stressful for a lot of people. Exceeding your customers' expectations assumes you have clarity about those expectations. How well do you understand your customers' current and future needs and/or hot buttons?

Over time, to literally have customers raving about the consistent manner in which your employees exceed their expectations elevates your company's brand to the rank of dominance. When you achieve that level of customers raving about you, you can oftentimes reduce your marketing and advertising budget, which also increases your profitability.

Being different doesn't have to be complicated. There is a plumber in Fort Myers, Florida, who built an entire marketing campaign and a business growth model around answering the phone. The company has grown threefold on that premise! You will never call between 8 a.m. and 8 p.m. without speaking to a real, live person within three rings. They've differentiated themselves and they keep growing. This plumbing company is not the cheapest in town, either.

Then the business owner added another part to the differentiation concept. Once the company sets up an appointment with you, if their plumber is not on site within 30 minutes, they'll take $10 off the cost of service for every minute they're late! Naturally, people can't stop telling others about this plumbing company. They do simple things like answer the phone and show up when they tell you they're going to show up. As you can see, some of these ideas do not take a great deal of ingenuity.

In 1999, Oakwood Healthcare selected a customer hot button—the wait time in the emergency rooms—as a way to generate more revenue by being different. The system's largest hospital, Oakwood Hospital, kicked off a strategy to significantly improve the delivery of ER services to its patients and to dramatically increase the volume of emergency care as part of Oakwood's overall business.

Within six months, Oakwood's emergency room had gone from a packed waiting room where people would routinely wait hours to see a doctor, to a guaranteed 30-minutes-or-less wait for physician evaluation. Before the project started, individuals and ambulances would often pass the Oakwood emergency room by in favor of other local hospitals. However, with the successful implementation of the Emergency Care System initiative, Oakwood became an industry leader for efficient emergency care that now draws people daily from the service areas of neighboring hospitals. Imagine the management commitment 18 months earlier to reinvent the way the entire hospital must operate to make that 30-minute guarantee. Every single department was involved to make the system faster and more efficient. That success translated into more admissions and revenues for the entire hospital system.

The mission at Southwest Airlines is simple: At Southwest Airlines, employees are our first customer. Think about it ... If your employees are not happy, how can they put on a happy face and deliver great customer service?
—Herb Kelleher, CEO, Chairman of Southwest Airlines

External Customer Satisfaction Is an Inside Job

So how does all of this tie in to employees? The employee experience is important because they're the ones who deliver your product. They're the ones who touch your customers every day, whether it's through an email, a phone call, a voice message, or processing an order.

Recently at a leadership round table event, I asked Todd Hohauser, the CEO of Harvey Hohauser & Associates, a top executive search firm, about workplace culture. He gave this definition: "learned and shared patterns of behavior, distinctive characteristics and beliefs of that group, and the goods, services, and tools shared with that group." Who owns the culture of your organization? The answer is everyone and no one. The environmental organism creates a mindset, a tempo, and rules that permeate the organization.

I asked Hohauser how important culture is when they partner with CEOs to conduct retained searches to recruit high-performing executives. According to Hohauser, executives "who fit into the culture or mindset thrive and succeed; those who don't are removed or severed from the culture." Likewise, he points out, if your strategy is not aligned with your culture, it will fail. "The companies we work with," Hohauser said, "that have the most successful, strong, and rewarding cultures, spend time on their values often. Leaders of the organization use corporate values to help define their culture, make decisions, and nurture and lead their direct reports. These are not just words on a poster on a wall, they are values that are revisited every day, week, or month. Use these values when recruiting talent."

I've said it before, but it bears repeating: how leaders treat employees is how employees treat customers, so why wouldn't you create systems to recognize people who go above and beyond? A magnetic culture attracts and retains top talent. When there's not enough great talent to go around, really great employees prefer to work at a place where they're treated with respect and dignity, where they're allowed to grow and develop as employees and associates, where there are promotional opportunities, if somebody goes above and beyond.

People like to work at a place where their voice is heard. If you study great places to work, you'll find places where they measure the culture of their workforce and associates are engaged. They ask employees for their input: "How can we make this a better place to work?" Regardless of whether it's a hospital, a manufacturing plant, or an office environment, people like to work at a place where every day seems like a Friday.

Have you ever noticed what employees are like the day before they go on vacation? Their title doesn't matter; it doesn't matter if they're a vice president or a director or if they drive a forklift on a shipping dock. They have a spring in their step, a smile on their face, and they tend to get things done quickly. They're just in a different frame of mind. They come to work looking forward to the next day when they go on vacation.

What if your workplace, your work unit, your division of the hospital, your section of the manufacturing plant, could create that kind of environment, where everyday associates at all levels in the organization gave you their discretionary effort, that little extra 5 or 10 percent? Yes, they have it, but unfortunately, over time, for many of them it's been suppressed. You didn't hire them that way. Your culture kind of molded them to be who they are today.

So the question becomes, how do you revive that energy in the workplace? It starts with your leadership team. It's all about making your company a fun place to work. It doesn't matter what kind of business you operate. Make it a place where people look forward to coming to work every day. While it takes work and dedication, it starts with the right management team. You can create that kind of work environment. In most companies, there is generally some percentage of leaders who become role models and create that type of work unit.

Remember, you only have four options: tolerate your current management team, buy new talent, develop the talent you already have, or a combination of buying new talent and developing your current talent.

When we talk about your internal and external customers, what role does trust play in your culture? Trust seems to be an interesting and provoking word in the workplace. The CEO must trust his or her direct reports. Customers must trust that a company will deliver its product or service. Vendors must trust that they will be paid on time. Employees must trust one another. Employees must trust that they will have a future and a career at the company. They must trust that bad apple employees will be dealt with and that top performers will be moved up the corporate ladder. All trust issues (and there are many more examples) are components of a culture.

What happens when trust is violated or inconsistent or simply nonexistent in your company? What happens when employees cannot trust management? What happens when an employee cannot trust their manager? You will find an organization filled with people who simply come to work and do their job, never anything more and occasionally something less. If you're the CEO, you have a dangerous future ahead of you, if you've lost people's excitement about coming to work, that extra discretionary effort.

Any discussion around your leaders creating the right culture should be directly targeted at your customers' experiences, which is the end result. Culture is a real, palpable, and measurable component that predisposes a company to either optimal or degraded performance overall. By systematically analyzing companywide activities in relation to culture, you will soon come to realize where the breakdowns occur between your strategy and your operations. Culture will trump strategy every time. It does not matter how detailed your strategic planning efforts are, your culture will determine your ability to execute your plans.

"Understanding and aligning culture prior to recruiting any executive is paramount to successfully completing an executive recruitment project," says Todd Hohauser. Prior to recruiting or presenting any candidates to the organization, a complete environmental audit of your organization needs to be completed. What type of people succeed within your organization? Did they attend certain schools? Do they have a particular personality or behavioral makeup (e.g., such as those determined by Hogan assessments, Profiles XT, Myers-Briggs or DISC assessments)? This alignment," Hohauser explains, "ensures the correct match is made to your culture. The correct match can catapult your organization to success and growth, while an incorrect match can be devastatingly expensive."

Hohauser recommends you use these values when recruiting talent. "We have recruited and secured the most amazing, high-performance executives for our clients," Hohauser states. "Some professionals look good on paper, present well, and have achievements and substance, but they do not match the culture. When candidates and/or employers ignore these cultural mismatch red flags, no one wins."

However, when the right match is made, Hohauser claims magic can happen. "We had a client that purchased a company for $800,000.00, a technology business with a small group of smart employees. After helping them staff their management team, they were able to grow in five years and sell the company for $80 million. Not a bad return!"

Build It, They Are Coming

We've been talking about customers and how your company culture can make your business stand out from the others. In general, it boils down to price, product, or service. But think about this: What if you could take your current level of service and effortlessly kick it up a few notches? And what if you could add a new, creative, out-of-the-box way of thinking that was so technologically savvy, it would put you miles ahead of your competitors? It sounds great, doesn't it? Well, there's an opportunity to do just that and it's accessible now. It's literally just right around the corner. Enter the millennials!

Millennials have a lot to offer. They are not only extremely comfortable in a technological world, they embrace it. After all, they don't know anything else. These racially diverse, young workers pride themselves on being tech-savvy, socially interconnected, and collaborative. Add the fact that baby boomers are retiring by the day, and it becomes clear that the workplace pipeline needs to be kept full, if your company is to continue and thrive. Also impacting your talent pipeline is the fact that many baby boomers are staying in the workplace longer than originally expected. That translates to three different generations making up your workforce. Granted, the three generations don't necessarily think alike, but having them present opens up a lot of discussions, which equates to new ideas.

Most likely you've heard a lot of negatives about the millennials, including their reputation for being self-centered, materialistic, spoiled, impatient, and entitled. Take a closer look and there may be some good reasons for the well-defined "attitude" they exhibit. First, they have the numbers on their side, as 50 percent of the world's population is under the age of 30. That's a huge factor. Another enormous factor, one that I just mentioned, is that they are into all things digital. They are the first generation born into a digital world. As a result, their entire lives are public record and visible on social networks. This can't help but impact their behaviors, attitudes, and expectations, especially when it comes to the workplace and dealing with employers. But, their pride in their intellect and social consciousness outweigh the negatives and are a real plus.

Culture can change and adapt over time, Hohauser maintains. In seeking to align your organization to the millennial workforce, ask your millennial employees, "What do you enjoy about working here? Why do you work here?" Once you uncover these key points, be certain to follow up, implement, or augment their suggestions. Doing nothing will turn them off and send them quickly out of your organization, Hohauser says.

The fact is, the millennials will form a significant portion of the workforce in the next three to five years, and signs of them actively shaping the workforce culture and expectations can already be seen. What does that mean for corporations? Simply put, it means that you can't afford to be left behind. But be forewarned, there is an "art" to attracting and retaining millennials. It takes a little research and an understanding of this tech-savvy social generation to hone the "art." The corporate culture has to be socially conscious, flexible, conducive to open communications and idea sharing, and "cool."

Take a hard look at your current corporate culture. Millennials continually ask what their company is doing for them. If they don't feel that the value of the company is stellar, then they simply move on to the next opportunity. Businesses can't continue to allow that to happen. These tech-savvy employees can guarantee that your company remains on the cutting-edge. Look at the numbers again . . . there are approximately 80 million millennials who could make up 36 percent of the U.S. workforce next year. By 2020, they could approach 50 percent of the workforce. They are the most educated and culturally diverse of all previous generations. On the negative side, they are already gaining the reputation as being "job hoppers" who dislike bureaucracy and distrust hierarchies.

When building the physical side of the corporate culture, research is an important factor. Yet few companies have done their homework. If you look at the companies who have incorporated millennial-friendly design, it's easy to see why their retention success rate is worlds above the rest.

Take Kcrua (www.kcrua.com), a Chicago-based company building web-based software that manages large volumes of electronic evidence during litigation or investigations. Kcrua's 330-person office is voluminous, spanning 76,000 square feet. Kcura didn't design its new office to attract a young workforce, but says it did pay attention to its employees, more than half of which are millennials. Preparing to move its offices, they enlisted the architecture firm Gensler to observe the way employees worked for three months before creating the new design. The results were just what millennials love—an expansive, colorful office covered in white boards, abundant breakout spaces, and a mess hall type of "town hall" room.

Perhaps the most important change that companies need to integrate into their culture is the changing role of leadership and how it reacts to and interacts with their millennials. Leadership will have to take a hard look at itself and initiate change in order to retain millennials and thrive. Millennials want to take the fast track to success and aren't willing to wait too long for promotions. Typically, organizations have less difficulty retaining employees in a bad economy. However, as the economy improves, more employment opportunities are sure to arise.

Millennials are unique. They're smart and should be a welcome addition to your company. Knowing what attracts them will help you know how to keep them. Think of them and other top performers as your greatest asset, and treat them as a company wellness plan—a well-designed talent recruitment and retention system that impacts every key area of your operation, and when properly utilized, will keep your company running like a well-oiled machine.

Study this list, but focus on the question below it. Millennials expect that you will:

1. Make work more meaningful and fun
2. Design your workplace to be modern, colorful, and not boring
3. Have a company that is socially engaged and gives back
4. Engage each employee as an individual (they do not like to be bored)
5. Create challenging work assignments
6. Deal with and/or eliminate poor performers
7. Help them professionally to grow and develop
8. Provide timely face-to-face feedback
9. Have a company with clear vision and a sense of purpose
10. Assist them in finding meaning and impact in their work
11. Have a strong commitment to developing a top-performing leadership team at all levels
12. Make them feel both welcome and appreciated
13. Provide recognition in front of management
14. Frequently encourage and support them in building their career
15. Have an onboarding system (they expect you are ready to integrate them quickly as a new hire into your culture)

16. Have a leadership team that demonstrates a management style that is engaging and personal, especially including work-life balance
17. Listen to their ideas
18. Role model your company values every day
19. Have leaders who communicate with candor and transparency
20. Budget for and demonstrate that education and development is a priority for all staff
21. Consistently update or eliminate stiff bureaucracy and/or outdated policies
22. Create opportunities for workplace flexibility
23. Train all managers to be great mentors and coaches
24. Collaborate and look for new positions to expand their growth
25. Involve them in planning and executing volunteer projects regularly
26. Encourage entrepreneurial thinking and actions

A challenging question: *Don't all top performers, regardless of age, expect what's outlined in the above list?*

This brings us back full circle to the concept of corporate culture. Is yours healthy? Are you and your leadership willing to adapt or to modernize it? Knowing the health status of your culture is possibly one of the most important things leadership needs to be aware of. It's your company's personality . . . its heart and soul. It's that important. It's a way for leadership, supervisors, and employees to interact in a way that benefits everyone and makes the company strong.

Getting Serious about Your Company's Culture

It's often amazing to hear what's said when I ask employees and managers to confidentially write down several words to describe their workplace culture. I've asked thousands of people to write down just two or three of the first words that come to mind. The response I receive borders on being embarrassing. There are some very positive words, but there are an awful lot of words that are upsetting to executives. Below are some descriptive words from 20 managers who were recently asked to describe the culture in their company:

Positive Words	Negative Words
Smart people	Stressed
Desire to do great work	Overworked
Inspired	Communication
Goal-oriented	Lack of focus
Innovation	Quality slipping
Fast-paced	Excess meetings
Results driven	Turnover
People/talent	Firefighting
Opportunities	Inefficient
Rewards	Too many average people

Would it be valuable to know what your employees think? Just how do you measure culture? Try asking! All it takes is for the CEO to have the wisdom and the courage to bring in an external company that has a culture assessment tool that can be used to solicit feedback from every employee in your company, including vice presidents.

But before you get started, effective culture assessment systems usually require a large amount of strategic upfront preparation and communication to your workforce. In most cases, an associate can complete a culture assessment in 20 to 25 minutes. The step that many executives skip or do not take seriously is the upfront communication before the survey, and without preparing the organization for the assessment, without that proper positioning, many organizations falter. They simply instruct people to complete the survey and leave it at that.

Most of the time in those circumstances, in those companies, there are negative scores, which are a reflection of how annoyed people are that once again management has made us complete this stupid cultural survey, and oh, by the way, you didn't do anything with it last time we completed it. That's the second biggest problem with culture assessments for executives.

At the end of the day, that's a CEO's responsibility. Shame on you, if you ask your employees to tell you what it's like to work at your company and you don't have any communication and action plan in place to do something with the survey results, including going back to people in a relatively quick manner and telling them about your findings.

This brings the issue of trust to the forefront, before attempting to ask your employees to participate in yet another survey. It's a fact that overall trust in leaders and leadership is declining. And there may be good reason for that. Remember Watergate? Junk bonds? Enron? The list goes on. In short, the attitude of "trust no one" has become widespread. This attitude carries over to the workplace and customer base, where a lack of trust in management and leadership is still evident.

How can it be fixed? Richard Edelman of Edelman, the world's largest public relations firm, suggests that today businesses can build trust by treating employees well, exhibiting ethical and transparent practices, and placing customers ahead of profits, while also delivering quality products and services. Corporate reputations have taken a hit, but they can recover by following the examples of a new breed of leaders who are exhibiting a far more effective leadership style, thus earning trust across the board. This new breed of leaders is demonstrating five key qualities, as laid out by Jeffrey Sonnenfield, Associate Dean of Yale School of Management. He breaks it down as follows:

- ☐ Personal dynamism and accessibility
- ☐ Empathy and concern
- ☐ Moral authenticity
- ☐ Inspirational goals
- ☐ Personal courage

Times have changed and that means the rules have changed. Employees want the truth. This new breed of empowered employees wants to feel included. They want to know what is expected of them. They want to excel and be given opportunities to grow into new roles and responsibilities. This reinforces the fact that corporate culture has got to change in order to succeed. You can conduct surveys ad nauseam. The reality is that leadership has to ask honest questions in their surveys, and they have to be prepared to react and act on the answers. You can look at this as the first step in building trust.

Leadership is asking more and more of their employees these days. It can easily be misconstrued as being taken advantage of. What's the answer? Leaders have to instill a level of trust. They need to pay attention to their employees and show appreciation. They need to listen to suggestions and grievances, and then come up with answers and act on those answers.

Now factor in your new group of millennials. They will not remain in a position where they don't feel appreciated or where there is a lack of trust in leadership. They are forthcoming and happy to give input. But they expect to be listened to and have their ideas or suggestions taken seriously. That doesn't mean that leadership has to agree with them, but it does mean that leadership has to be honest with their responses and reactions and be able to back that up with facts.

In the article "Seven Reasons Employees Don't Trust Their Leaders" on Forbes.com, Glenn Llopis talks about the trust issues with leadership and employees. He highlights Nelson Mandela as an example of trusted leadership and reminds us that the great leaders of the world gravitated to Mandela because of his trustworthiness and genuineness. Here are Llopis's seven early warning signs of trust in leadership breaking down, which are well worth considering:

☐ **Lack Courage**
Leaders that don't stand up for what they believe in are hard to respect and trust.
☐ **Hidden Agendas**
There is a universal distrust in politics and politicians. Leaders that are too politically savvy can be viewed as devious and inauthentic.
☐ **Self-Centered**
Hidden agendas make it difficult to trust the leader's intentions.

- ☐ **Reputation Issues**
  Negative conversations about a leader make it difficult to trust their intentions and vision.
- ☐ **Inconsistent Behavior**
  It's human nature that people are inclined to trust those whose behavior is consistent.
- ☐ **Don't Get Their Hands Dirty**
  Leaders must not only lead, they must be involved in the business.
- ☐ **Lack a Generous Purpose**
  If it looks like a leader doesn't have your best interests at heart, it's really difficult to trust them.

Today's leaders must find ways to enhance or regain the trust of their employees. The corporate culture has to focus less on the leaders and more on the whole. The results will be a more cohesive and productive workplace. Engagement surveys are a great tool to solicit ideas for improvement, to show you care, and to enhance trust in your company.

Actions Speak Louder Than Surveys

It's evident that the issue of trust must be dealt with prior to any official communications or surveys taking place. The opportunity, or the challenge, for most CEOs is not completing the survey itself, that's the easy part. Where most CEOs need to pay attention is the thoroughness of their communication, focusing on preparing and positioning the organization before the survey is taken. In most companies, a special all management meeting can significantly improve the participation of associates in your culture survey. Managers must be able to communicate inside their departments as to why people are being asked for their honest opinions. So preparing the organization to complete the assessment comes first. Completing the assessment is second. Communicating and taking action on the survey results is appropriately the third step in the process.

If you don't prepare the organization properly, you'll get garbage feedback from your survey. You won't end up with good results if people show up ticked off because of how they were simply mandated to take the survey. Managers at every level must be briefed, trained, and instructed in how to include and engage their direct reports to volunteer to complete the survey, that's right, volunteer. If a company has taken surveys in the past and has not had great success with them, the preparation or the followup is usually the problem. Survey results that come from associates who are mandated or told to complete it are rarely effective or honest. They usually take that opportunity to whine or complain, and the feedback is skewed.

So managers usually need guidance in coaching and/or training on how to solicit employees to volunteer to take the company survey, especially if 40-50 percent of your managers are "C" performers now. Then, once employees complete the survey properly with the right mindset, magic starts to happen. It has to do with how you respond to the culture survey results.

First, you should put together an executive summary signed by the CEO or the executive team and send it to every single associate in the company. You should provide people with feedback that says, "Here are the strengths of the organization through your eyes, and here are some challenges and things we need to get better at. Thank you for your honest feedback. Action planning will get underway soon."

The next phase of action you should take as an executive team is for your leaders and executives to be role models and hold their direct reports accountable to actually do something with the survey results. Then those same managers and directors need to hold frontline supervisors accountable for taking action as well.

If you're going to take a culture survey and follow it up with action on the results, and do it properly and periodically, which you should, how well have you trained your entire management team to do so effectively? Is developing talent an organizational imperative at your company? If not, you're undoubtedly missing opportunities to convert your internal customer base into an effective and committed brand.

If you recall a statistic I cited earlier, high performers generate

48 to 128 percent higher revenue than average performers. Great places to work tend to attract top-performing, great employees. It's true in sports. Great teams tend to attract more great free agents to join their team. People like to win. They like coming to a place where they enjoy working.

What if you had an organization filled with really great performers? What if you stopped tolerating mediocrity from some of your workers? What if you eliminated all "D" performers six months from now? Then you spend the next 12 months elevating a lot of your "C" performers to "B" performers. What if you filled your organization with people who are that talented and passionate? What kind of an impact would that have on your organization's ability to attract and retain great people?

Remember what was stated earlier about why CEOs fail. They don't fail due to bad strategy; they fail because of their inability to execute. That's the number one reason for CEO termination, according to an article in *Fortune*. Your company's ability to execute is directly tied to your ability to touch your customers in a different way, so you'll stand out from your competitors, including in your profitability. Execution is all about your delivery model to the customer, your ability to fulfill your promise. Every business has two fundamental responsibilities: to land customers and to deliver on their promise. It doesn't matter if you're a car dealership selling a car, a roofer putting a new roof on a house, or a department store selling lots of different items. You've got to get customers and then you've got to deliver.

So serving your customers optimally still comes down to execution. Failure to execute oftentimes means you don't have the right leaders in the right place, you don't have leaders with the right talent, and you don't have everybody in the organization aligned. You also may not have an effective accountability system, because your ability to execute really is your ability to deliver on your promise to the customer.

CHAPTER 9

What's Stopping You from Developing Your Leadership Talent?

Each breakthrough company was surrounded by a network of outside resources vital to its success. We call these resources "scaffolding" because, like physical scaffolding, these outside experts are temporary structures that exist outside of the organization itself and enable the company to get to the next level.

—Keith R. McFarland, *The Breakthrough Company*

Who will use the information in this book and who won't? Are you one of the 22 percent? Are you one of the few who will take action on the information you've read here?

Very early in this book, I referenced the fact that readers will fall into one of three categories: the 8 percent of executives at the top of their industry, the 22 percent in the middle who have been trying to improve, and the 70 percent who are satisfied with the status quo. You can see that breakdown in Figure 10.

That 8 percent, they're the industry leaders right now. They've already implemented the majority of the solutions presented here. They run the companies others want to visit to see what they're doing. People are writing stories about them.

The 22 percent in the middle want to get to the top. They've been experimenting with different concepts, tried a consulting firm, and are trying to make some changes, but they're just not there yet. They

Figure 10

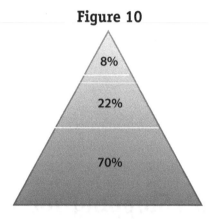

next level. For them, it's a matter of learning the best strategies for their company, developing their leadership team, getting the right plan, and then taking action.

That 70 percent are not even trying and will not reach the top. On balance, they have no hope for ever being an industry leader; they're going to have to accept mediocrity. I could mail this book to people in the 70 percent category and not one of them—in spite of all the success stories—would contact me to learn more about how I've assisted other companies in making significant improvements that have led to amazing results in employee and customer satisfaction, company growth, and profitability. They're just not interested in how I, or someone like me, could help them do the same inside their organization.

So what holds CEOs and companies back from making the changes necessary to move their company to the top of their industry? Why is it so hard to change? There are a few reasons, but those I most commonly come across are arrogance, the CEO thinks he/she knows what they're doing, and closed-mindedness. They're just not open to outside best practices.

In some cases, they think their human resources director or department head or vice president of human resources has everything under control. Or there's no real sense of urgency; nothing is driving the change, so sometimes executives become complacent with the way the company is running. Simply stated, too many business owners or executives have become okay with "good" results and that is unfortunate.

Another major reason that companies don't move forward in embracing novel ideas has to do with a lack of clarity around a possible new vision for the organization. The CEO lacks the ability to see the company in a whole new light, to see it going from small, single-digit margins to growing, double-digit margins. Some executives just can't visualize, and that limiting belief becomes a barrier to big progress. And if you can't see it, how can you get others on board?

I must state that the owners of some mid-size, privately owned businesses are simply okay with their company's current situation. Life is good, and good is good enough. Some business owners fall into the cruise control category: they get into routines and habits that become a hamster on a wheel. Every day they are busy in their business and rarely step outside of it to investigate a new possibility. One example of a business's success is that it will run successfully for long periods of time without the owner. Will yours?

Finally, there are leaders who simply lack the courage to take the steps. Without the courage and the confidence to go find and model some best practices they could bring in to their company, executives just keep doing what they're doing and expect different results with their current leadership talent.

Talent is the natural capacity for excellence. People can learn skills, develop knowledge, and gain experience, but they cannot acquire talent—it is innate. Few leaders have the total package. Only 1 in 10 leaders have the high talent to effectively manage others. That means 1 in 10 will engage associates and customers, retain top talent, and build a high-performing culture.
—Gallup 2015 National Study

Master These Four Words for a Winning Combination

When people ask me what it takes to create a sustainably profitable company, and how they can differentiate their business from all the others in their industry, four words always come to mind: leadership, people, product, and systems. One solution you may be thinking about is putting better systems and processes in place. What would it take for your management team to be able to lead and facilitate the improvement and the implementation of systems and processes that help your organization execute consistently every time?

Regardless of the size of your company, it's to your benefit to implement systems and processes like that of a family-owned business or a franchise. There are over five million family-owned businesses in the United States today. They employ 63 percent of the American workforce, according to the Family Enterprise USA Study of 2012, and 75 percent of all new jobs are generated by family-owned businesses. If somebody is looking to buy a business in today's business world, buying a franchise usually is a good idea, because franchises have proven systems and processes.

Later in this chapter, we will also point out how meaningful systems are to position your business to run effectively and/or to prepare it for sale someday. A privately owned business with strong leadership, great people, systems that work, and a product and service model will usually sell for more money. Said differently, when the business runs very well without the owner, it is more attractive when it's for sale on the market.

So imagine if your business could become much more systemized and operate much more consistently. What would it take to move from where your business is today to run at that level? What would it take for business magazines to be writing stories about the turnaround of your company three to four years from now?

One of the most important systems related to people and talent that is poorly designed, trained, administered, and tolerated at far too high a level in organizations is how they deal with bad apples, or in this matter, underground resistance. By that I'm referring to resistance to change: the people who will stand in your way when you decide you're going to start doing things differently.

Find out just who is a great producer, who's an average producer, and who's a poor producer. What's interesting about this is that people already know who those slackers are. Any CEO can ask for some honest feedback and everybody in the organization could come up with three to 10 names of who in the company are the bad apples. They all know who those people are, and in many cases so do the vice presidents and department heads.

So why are they simply allowed to be on the payroll, if everybody knows they work really hard at doing as little as possible all day long? Why don't companies put a better system in place and train their managers? You have to have leaders holding leaders accountable to actually deal with this situation.

Many leaders have become tolerant of average-performing people at all levels in their company. To me, that's an indication of poor accountability, starting at the top. This is where leaders have to use their accountability system, because without an effective accountability system, what evidence would you have about who's a bad apple. This is one of the talent management systems we talked about in Chapter 5.

Here's a warning: Some of your underground resistors could be pretty average employees, not bad employees, but they've been around for a long time. Yet you've got to let them go. There's no room for underground resistance. They will fight everything you're trying to do in the organization to move forward. Unless your leadership team has the skill and the system and the courage to deal with underground resistors, your ability to move the needle on making your culture a great place to work will always be slowed down considerably. I have found this to be true in more than 70 percent of companies with which I have partnered.

Why aren't leaders held accountable to improve or delete all forms of resistance? Too many executives worry more about being popular and having people like them. They don't have the courage to make tough decisions and hold people accountable. I don't know how you can grow an organization and develop leaders without doing so, because without accountability, results are just a matter of luck.

The Real Power and Impact of Systems

There are many benefits to implementing effective systems and processes in your business, especially if the business is privately owned.

Your quality improves, morale goes up, work gets done faster, and internal communication is clearer. You also may oftentimes require less talented associates in many roles. If they can read and follow the system, they can do a very good job for you.

Most privately owned business CEOs do not fully appreciate the power and impact that well-written and followed systems can have on their business. Do you ever wonder why the world record for successfully solving a Rubik's Cube puzzle is under 11 seconds, or under 12 seconds for doing so one-handed? They have a system. It's the same reason entrepreneurs have a better chance of success if they buy a franchise—they are buying a proven, successful set of systems.

Let's define a "system." I refer to a system as a series of steps designed to achieve a specific outcome. The healthcare industry uses the word "process" instead of "system." Every company, regardless of size, is built with hundreds of systems. If the leaders are not systems experts, there can be a high risk of problems or breakdowns.

While all privately owned businesses have systems, some are more accurately called "the way we do things here." For example, if you want to know the system for how the company collects money, ask Logan. Unfortunately, Logan has 21 years of her habits and routines stored in her head, which makes it hard for someone else to follow when she goes on vacation or calls in sick or leaves for more money somewhere else. It's simply not a good business practice.

You need to keep a pulse on all the systems and their interconnected parts, if you don't want your business to flatline. Find your most common mistakes or areas where someone forgets to do something and get that system documented—quickly. Another great strategy is to first document all those systems that impact cash flow or the customer experience.

Why don't more business owners focus on their systems? That's the $1 million question. Regrettably, many do not know how vital these systems are to their bottom line. And, among those who do, many would rather avoid the painstaking and tedious task of documenting how to optimally perform every part of every job in the company. It makes no difference whether you own a Subway franchise or are an entrepreneur running a $10 million company, your business will operate more effectively if you have:

1. Identified all the systems essential to running your business
2. Documented every step of every system
3. Saved every system on a computer that is backed up daily
4. Tested the system for accuracy
5. Approved or have a subject matter expert sign off on rolling out the tested system
6. Trained every employee in how to maintain your profit generating systems
7. Empowered managers and leaders to hold people accountable for adhering to the systems
8. Provided positive feedback and recognition to those employees who do support and follow the systems related to their job performance

Both your body and your business need a finely tuned organizational alignment to operate effectively. In your business, this can only occur if you have an annual organizational plan that links job descriptions and performance expectations to the effective support and appreciation of the company's systems. Case in point: Investors Susan and Barbara McCarthy, former owners and founders of Sun Country Cleaners in St. Petersburg, Florida, were recognized nationally as the 2010 Enterprising Women Business Owners of the Year. The recognition came on the heels of them having surveyed their customer base as to the top reason they return to Sun Country for their cleaning needs: 5,000 people responded that it was the friendliness of the staff. That feedback was a critical step in the company's customer retention system and most likely one of the reasons they are one of the fastest growing dry cleaners in Florida.

Sun Country Cleaners remains committed to continue to improve its business performance. The company has a process in place to flag the leadership when a new problem pops up. Then a new system is developed to prevent the issue from repeating itself, and the appropriate employees know what to do should something similar occur.

In reality, you have a lot of what you consider to be systems already in place. However, unless you've done the requisite assessment, training, and documentation activities, your systems are likely a collection of habits, some good and some not so good. Systematic approaches will both defeat bad habits and instill good quality habits in the working structure of your business.

Do what your competition probably won't: Think about your systems long before they have a chance to break down or disappoint a customer. To get started, create an effective one-year master plan, map out your most frequently used systems, or those systems which most consistently impact your customers and/or profitability and cash flow first. Think of this master plan as a success wellness plan. A well-designed collection of systems orchestrating every core part of your operations will have your organization running like a well-oiled machine, with associates making fewer mistakes. Stress and anxiety are reduced for staff, too. I have seen organizations improve productivity and/or decrease quality errors by as much as 15-20 percent annually by significantly increasing the focus on systems administration.

In addition, onboarding and training staff becomes easier. If systems and processes are fully implemented, it no longer looks like someone new watching a current employee do the work. Systems and processes are always subject to improvement, which for many companies becomes one of the organization's values—continuous improvement. One additional benefit to a systems designed company is that the organization is simply more productive, and that can save overtime dollars for many companies.

Staging Your Business to Sell

There are many ways for a business owner to leverage the principles in this book. One of the applications of these learnings has to do with building a company in the private sector that can be sold for the highest multiple possible. If in 2015 and beyond, more and more companies are listed for sale, only the best-built companies will sell for the highest price possible. So consider the possibility of selling your business to a private equity group or a strategic buyer. How prepared or staged is your business when they venture on site and start peeking under the rocks? The following are some rocks under which they will look:

1. How has your business performed financially over the last three years?
2. How well will the business run without the owner?
3. How strong is your management team?
4. How effective are your systems/processes?
5. How effective is your marketing machine and/or sales compared to your competition?
6. What is your growth potential?
7. What is your industry forecast?
8. What is your customer retention like and how diversified is your customer base?
9. What is your cost and margin structure?

The possibility of someday selling your business might be the motive you need to start developing your management team now, especially since eight of the nine factors above are directly impacted by the quality and effectiveness of your management team. Whether you're looking for cash to expedite your growth, looking to acquire compatible companies that may bolt on to your business, or simply want to sell a percentage of your company to an outside investment group, growth is substantially easier and more profitable if your company is filled with great talent and if you have implemented the hundreds of systems required for quality, speed, and overall effectiveness. Regardless of your approach, if you attempt to grow your company without great talent and systems, I can promise you that you will experience tremendous chaos, and your employees, your customers, and your cash flow will be impacted negatively.

We had come to a crossroads in our business: We had ramped up our sales force but were in desperate need to produce a quality result for our clients and customers. We consulted with Premier Executive Forums in 2012 and successfully implemented a plethora of systems, processes, and protocols. In our first year after implementation, we grew our top-line revenue by 53.7% for the year. This year we are on track to close 127.5% more residential mortgages than we did in 2013. We could not have grown that fast without our focus on systems implementation.

—**Kevin Broughton, Success Mortgage Partners**

Have the Courage and Discipline to Stick with Your Plan

There are five fundamental keys to the ongoing execution of your operational plan: effective leadership, alignment, accountability, the right talent, and proper systems and processes. However, you can't have systems and processes running smoothly unless you have those other components of the blueprint in place.

When I talk to leaders inside organizations, they rarely see themselves as part of the problem. One of the reasons is that they don't get very accurate feedback, so leaders don't realize they're part of the problem. If properly facilitated, if properly designed, if properly introduced, conducting a leadership assessment on people in leadership positions is key to all execution issues.

Most leaders are not very good at providing effective coaching or feedback, so unless you have some type of a process, a leadership assessment, or a confidential 360 Survey assessment, how would managers receive any kind of feedback, other than the compliments they get from their boss occasionally? Without accurate feedback, how would they know?

Probably the single biggest mistake executives make is that they do not take action with average or underperforming managers. Generally speaking, they do a poor job of holding leaders accountable. Talk about the glue that holds it all together: If the CEO can't hold vice presidents accountable, and if vice presidents cannot hold their department heads and directors accountable, and they won't hold frontline supervisors and team leaders accountable, accountability in the company will be a joke. If you currently have a review system, there is a high probability that managers' reviews will be inflated; they will not reflect the actual performance of their department or unit, or for that matter the company's overall performance. You cannot start that process of implementing the strategies that will make your company a top performer without having the right leadership talent throughout your organization. And you need to make them accountable.

By now you should be asking yourself, how does my company become the best? How do I take my business from where it is today to becoming an industry leader? One of the things you can do is to make the best use of outside resources to support your climb to the top. Do you, as a CEO, really understand how to do that? You may already use outside experts like CPAs to do audits, and external legal counsel for human resource issues or mergers and acquisitions. So why wouldn't you bring in a leadership development expert to help you begin to shape the direction of how your company thinks about current and future leaders?

If there were a mirror in this chapter, I'd ask you to take a hard look at yourself, because that's where it starts. It's a personal decision on the part of the CEO. A decision only takes a half second to make. But sometimes it takes a CEO or an executive team years to be ready to make that decision, then have the courage and the discipline to stay the course once a blueprint has been laid out for where they want to take the company in the next three to five years.

If you read this book, put it on a shelf, and do nothing different, nothing will fundamentally change. Right now you should be questioning your motivation to change. At the same time, you should be questioning your reluctance to change, because at the heart and soul of all this is your willingness to do what it takes to change.

Are you willing to be the change leader in your company? If you knew what to do, would you do it? Would changing the direction and the financial future of your company get you excited? What if you decided to make developing your leadership team a business priority?

And what if your top two competitors call me and you don't?

CHAPTER 10

Do You Now Have the Answers for Your Business?

Research has also shown that engaged organizations have 56% higher customer loyalty, are 50% more productive, and 33% more profitable, and have a 44% higher retention rate.

—Marcus Buckingham and D. Clifton,
First, Break All the Rules

There is a leadership drought in America today. Far too many executives stopped developing and/or training their current and future leaders over the last five to seven years. One of the implications of that shortsighted decision is that top-performing leaders are going to have choices about where they work; many executives will begin to search elsewhere. And beware, your top leadership talent is being contacted by executive recruiters.

Recently, in a conversation with Todd Hohauser, he shared with me that "as the economy picks up momentum, many CEOs have the need to expand their management teams to better serve their customers and expand their product/service/goods offering. Funding is available and hiring executives has gathered momentum. Owners of companies are more focused on finding executives that match their culture. Knowledge, skills, and abilities are not a panacea for success; there MUST be alignment with executive candidates and the culture of the organization they will be joining. Leadership qualities, the ability to mentor and nurture up and coming performers, is in high demand. Those executives that have demonstrated abilities to inspire and motivate will be quickly employed, promoted, and recruited."

Hohauser continued, "Leaders are being pulled in so many directions today, they need support—support from their organization, from their owners, and from their direct reports. If they are not getting support from their employers, they are leaving. High-performing candidates that are NOT acknowledged either verbally or financially are moving to companies that will give them that recognition. The number one reason people leave jobs is their boss. If there is not alignment with the culture and their boss, they will leave to find a better fit." And if you need more proof, "more than 7,200 adults confirmed their number one reason for leaving the company was their immediate manager," according to *Gallup's 2015 National American Manager Study.*

Really talented leaders want to win, and they will leave organizations that do not meet their expectations. The Gallup 2013 study, "The State of the American Workplace: Employee Engagement Insights for U.S. Business Leaders Report," found that talented leaders want to work inside cultures that are creating cultures where engagement is measured and constantly improving. Employee engagement is one of the leading indicators of effective leadership. With such alarming new research below, the Gallup organization is again pointing out the business case for strategically developing leaders. And of the approximately 100 million people in America who hold full-time jobs, only 30 million (30 percent) are engaged and inspired at work.

The Results for 2015 Are In

In 2015, the results have not changed. Gallup again studied performance at hundreds of organizations and measured the engagement of 27 million employees and more than 2.5 million work units over the past two decades. The number one finding again in 2015 was that only 30 percent of the employees surveyed were actually engaged. The 2015 Gallup study reported that:

- ☐ Managers account for at least 70 percent of the variance in employee engagement.
- ☐ Companies fail to choose the management candidate with the right talent for the job 82 percent of the time.
- ☐ Employees whose managers are open and approachable are more engaged.
- ☐ Employees whose managers help them set work priorities and goals are more engaged.
- ☐ Managers who work for engaged leaders are 39 percent more likely to be engaged.
- ☐ Employees who work for engaged managers are 59 percent more likely to be engaged.
- ☐ Managers with high talent are twice as likely to be engaged.

If you are not measuring your culture's engagement, you should be. But remember, you must be equally committed to taking action with the survey results.

Every organization should have its own leadership development process and system, and most organizations do not. That was my hypothesis at the beginning of this book. I set out to prove to you that you need to be spending a lot more time and energy developing your leadership team, and that you need to be taking a strategic approach to doing so. My challenge was to explain to you why leadership development is, perhaps, the single greatest factor that can determine your company's current and future financial condition.

By now I've either gotten your attention and have proven my point (based on my own experience and research from other sources), or you'll stay as one of those CEOs in the 70 percent category. If you weren't aware of the enormous difference leadership development can make in your organization, you are now. You should be acutely aware of the need for a more systematic method for developing the current and future leaders at all three levels in your organization—senior leaders, middle management, and frontline leaders.

To run a top-performing company, to be a leader at any level in an organization, requires a significant difference in performance that directly ties to skill level and business knowledge. I find great leaders are awesome at making complicated things simple for people. They're fair and honest and motivating. They bring positive energy to the workplace, yet they're demanding.

As Warren Buffet once said, "You have to be willing to be different." Leaders today not only have to be able to see today and talk about today, they have to be able to talk about the future, to communicate their vision. They have to be able to articulate the direction the company is going in and why. It's that ability to see around corners, to be able to forecast and anticipate, and to inspire their employees.

How Is Your Management Team Really Doing?

Listed below are the critical questions you should ask yourself to assess your current management team and determine if they should be part of your company's future.

1. What percentage of your entire management team would you rehire as top performers, if you had to start all over again?

2. How many members of your management team can articulate their top four measurable priorities for this current calendar year?

3. What would it mean to your company's profitability in the next two or three years to become an industry leader in your market?

4. What words would your employees use to describe your current culture?

5. How exciting would it be to conduct a complete management assessment and identify which members of your management team should be in those key seats today and in the future?

6. On a scale of 1 to 10, with 10 being outstanding, what grade would you give your management team on how well they currently use your accountability system to align and monitor the performance of your company?

7. How well does your company eliminate poor or underperforming associates at all levels?

8. What percentage of your entire workforce is an "A" or "B" performer, or above average?

9. What percentage of your company's budget is devoted to systematically developing your entire management team?

10. How would it impact your company's customer experiences if your company culture truly provided a great place to work?

11. How effectively have you leveraged outside leadership development experts prior to now?

You should be starting to realize that some of your business challenges, if you get to the root cause, may be due to the fact you don't have as strong and talented a management team to execute as you thought you did. Too many of them are average, regardless of what you have done to date. Every component of your business strategy changes when you only have "A" and "B" performers on your management team.

Avoidable Leadership Mistakes Companies Make

The intent of this book was to share with you my 30-plus years of experiences developing leaders, with the sole purpose to improve the financial performance of your business. Regardless of whether your business is public or private, this book has attempted to provide you with the business rational and solutions to become an industry leader.

In addition to business solutions, below are a few common mistakes that I felt compelled to share with you because, in part, they are so frequently violated and the consequences are substantial. These are six powerful leadership mistakes that you, as a reader of this book, will know how to avoid, if you take the correct actions.

1. **Promoting leaders for the wrong reasons**

   Leaders at all levels are often promoted from one level in the organization to the next because of how well they're liked and how well they perform in their current job, not because they possess the skills and knowledge to perform at the next level in the organization. That's an erroneous assumption.

2. **Having no accurate descriptions of what real, top-performing leaders look like**

   The wrong data is being used to promote talent and make decisions about the leaders who are being promoted in most organizations. Without even knowing it, decision-makers are clogging their leadership pipeline with people who may not be top performers at the next level, partly because their system for promoting talent is not well-designed. The real data should include 360 Survey evaluation information and updated job descriptions, including clarity about responsibilities and key performance metrics at all levels of management. Leveraging the right leadership assessments will also provide statistically valid data for making upcoming leadership decisions.

3. **Making incorrect and costly assumptions due to lack of preparation**

   The leadership development system inside most companies is not forward or experiential thinking. It is simply assumed that every manager promoted is willing to learn and is capable of being a leader at the next level. Assumptions are made because there isn't a good process in place. People have to learn as they move up the company leadership ladder that there are different responsibilities, skills, and levels of complexity required. There's a learning curve, and most organizations don't prepare leaders for the next step.

4. **Tolerating poor performance**

   Far too many business owners and/or executives have become tolerant of managers at all three levels who are not top performers. Throughout this book, I've used the analogy of "A" performers, who are your rock stars; "B" performers, people who occasionally go above and beyond; and "C" performers or below, who are simply average performers that come to work, do their job, and go home. The facts are quite clear. If 30 to 50 percent of an organization's management team is average, it can't expect to be an industry-leading company with high profits. Remember, an organization will not outperform its management.

5. **Not devoting the time or money to design a leadership development program**
   Top-performing companies invest in their future. They may even create new positions as a development assignment, or provide executive education, executive coaching, and/or systematic leadership training for their current and future leaders. But too many CEOs are not willing to invest the time and the money to design an internal leadership development system. Then they wonder why their company is not doing better, not reaching goals, and not hitting profit targets.

6. **Assuming that developing current and future leaders is a human resource issue**
   Developing leaders is an executive issue, not something you assign to human resources. It's time to recognize that fact, take ownership, and take action!

Your current business performance is a direct reflection of your current management talent and its ability to execute. The above six mistakes are simply a combination of decisions you have made, consciously or not. By reading this book, you now have new options to consider. The question is your motive or desire to take your business to a whole new level, and whether are you willing to use outside experts to help you in areas that are not your strength. In his book *The Breakthrough Company,* regarding his research of America's 7,000 fastest growing private and public companies, Keith McFarland was quoted as saying that:

a. Only about a tenth of 1 percent (0.10 percent) of U.S. firms ever achieves revenues of more than $250 million in sales.

b. Breakthrough companies tend to be ruthless at prioritizing.

c. The best nine companies of the 7,000 had a willingness to go outside the company for help. The nine companies that had three times the profitably of their competitors were surrounded by a network of outside resources vital to their success.

How much proof do you need?

How You Can Strategically Change Your Current Situation

I told you at the beginning of this book that I was going to take you on a journey, a trip inside some of the best companies in America, so you could see what they do that you're not doing. Throughout this book, we've talked about solutions strategically mapped out as a blueprint, so you can assess your current talent and design your own leadership development system. To review, these are possible solutions that could change the future and direction of your company. These options are, in no particular order:

☐ Conduct an assessment of your leadership team at all three levels to determine if you have the right people in the right positions

☐ Form a committee to benchmark two or three other best practice companies and go study how they are doing it

☐ Launch your company's leadership development system

☐ Design a culture change movement committee

☐ Conduct a culture assessment

☐ Offer associates well-designed strategic training and development

☐ Evaluate your nine talent management systems

☐ Implement individual development plans (IDP) for every manager or leader at all three levels in your organization

☐ Conduct a 360 Survey feedback evaluation for everybody in management

☐ Launch your 5 percent planning system for annual, quarterly, and monthly meetings, right down to and including daily huddles

☐ Develop a leadership scorecard system

☐ Offer management training, a core leadership curriculum that's very strategically designed

☐ Offer executive coaching to help further and expedite the development of current and future high-potential leaders

☐ Redesign your performance management accountability system

☐ Eliminate underground resistors and/or poor performers

I don't understand why leaders will not invest in their company's future and develop talent that they already have. Before joining Allied-Signal, Larry Bossidy was vice chairman of General Electric and chief operations officer of GE Capital. When he joined AlliedSignal, one of his first priorities was to assess the individual talents of his management team. He made finding and developing leaders his top personal priority. He spent almost 40 percent of his time doing that.

When he joined AlliedSignal, stock prices were down, morale was down, and operating margins were below 5 percent. Nine years later, when they decided to merge with Honeywell, operating margins had almost tripled, and the return for shareholders was almost ninefold.

Just a Few Examples of the Results
John Lankford Has Helped Companies Achieve

A major wholesale flooring company opened a new retail showroom and was consistently showing a profit in less than 90 days.

Michigan's fastest growing mortgage company lost its COO and top three loan officers, yet had a 78% increase in revenues in one year and more than a 40% improvement in the next two years.

At the nation's largest communication company, one major call center exceeded its customer retention and growth targets by tenfold in a single calendar year.

Over a three-year period in one healthcare system:
- Organizational trust in management improved by 89%
- Employee satisfaction increased by 46%
- Turnover was reduced by 31%, contributing to an $8 million annual savings
- Communication between work teams on different shifts increased by 62%
- Customer service scores at multiple sites improved five times more than any other hospital or healthcare system in the country

One Big Three automotive manufacturer:
- Facilitated safety training to help reduce the accident/injury incident rate to a level that translated into a savings of over $10 million in a three-year period
- Had one "high-involvement" engine plant reduce its high-mileage warranty costs by $500 million in less than two years
- Had quality defects drop to 0 during one quarter in a manufacturing plant, a first for an automotive Big Three engine plant

Dozens of clients across America had tremendous financial growth, which translated into John winning the North American Business Advisor of the Year award in 2007-2010, based on his clients' results (four years in a row out of 450 offices in North America).

To find out more about John's results,
visit www.PremierExecutiveForums.com

Are You Committed to Greatness?

So, are you still wondering why your company isn't an industry-leading expert? Are you wondering why your margins are not where they should be? Are you wondering why your profitability is not where it needs to be, and there's a gap between how your company is performing, versus whoever is number one in your industry?

How willing are you to tolerate not being the best? Transitioning your company and resetting your company's path to sustained growth is possible, but something must change, and it starts with leadership. It comes down to assessing your current talent, making sure they are the right players for your team, and then committing to and doing everything you can to nurture that talent to the highest level possible. They win, your customers win, and of course, you win. Your company continues to grow and prosper, sustainably, as you reach the top of your industry.

Every executive who reads this book, fundamentally has four options when it comes to their company's leadership. Here's a reminder:

1. **Continue to tolerate the existing performance of your company and your current management team**
   You know the result of this option. It's not good.

2. **Hire an external executive search firm to fill your critical executive level openings**
   Using an executive search firm is your best option to fill openings. The reason why the executive search firm industry is growing so rapidly is because of the demand for top leadership talent. Perhaps the single biggest contributing factor is the lack of leadership development occurring in the private sector and/or corporate America.

3. **Develop your own leadership talent**
   This is the option I would recommend. At this point, you should understand why and how some of the greatest organizations in the world are developing their leadership talent.

4. **Some combination of numbers two and three**

So, are you going to continue to tolerate your management team's performance? Are you going to go out on the open market and buy new talent? Or will you make the decision to develop a plan to systemically evaluate and develop your own management team? In case you are wondering, it is quite common that after an assessment you may have some new decisions to make about your current leadership team's capabilities. When you consider the overall value that a top-performing executive brings to your company, you really must investigate partnering with a retained executive search firm to find and fill your next executive opening.

It's time to get real. It's time for you to make a serious decision about your company's future. Would you like to have a one-on-one conversation with me about your leadership team and your company's future? I invite you to contact me, right now, today, by phone or through my website. Pick up the phone and call me at 888-730-1950 or email me at john@PremierExecutiveForums.com for an initial consultation. Together, we can determine your best route to building a top-performing organization.

I hope this book has been educational and alarming. Are you in the 22 percent? If yes, take the next step to find out what might be possible for your company. Your answer will be yes if you have the courage to be uncomfortable for a short while. Remember, great leaders hate losing enough to change, while average leaders hate change enough to lose.

What are you doing to learn and grow as a leader each month?

Bibliography

American Society for Training and Development (ASTD). *ASTD 2012 State of the Industry Report: Organizations Continue to Invest in Workplace Learning.* ASTD, 2012. https://www.td.org/Publications/Magazines/TD/ TD-Archive/2012/11/ASTD-2012-State-of-the-Industry-Report.

Association for Talent Development (ATD). *2014 State of the Industry Report: Spending on Employee Training Remains a Priority.* Association for Talent Development, 2014. https://www.td.org/Publications/Magazines/TD/ TD-Archive/2014/11/2014-State-of-the-Industry-Report-Spending-on-Employee-Training-Remains-a-Priority.

Bartlett, Christopher A. and Sumantra Ghoshal. "Building Competitive Advantage through People." *MIT Sloan Management Review.* Winter 2002; January 15, 2002.

Bean, Jeofrey and Sean Van Tyne. *The Customer Experience Revolution: How Companies Like Apple, Amazon, and Starbucks Have Changed Business Forever.* St. Johnsbury, VT: Brigantine Media, 2011.

Borg, Tom. "How to Make Staff Pay for Itself." http://www.tomborgconsulting. com/make-staff-training-pay-2/.

Bossidy, Larry and Ram Charan. *Execution: The Discipline of Getting Things Done.* NY: Crown Business, 2002.

Buckingham, Markham and Curt Coffman. *First, Break All the Rules.* NY: Simon & Schuster, October 1999.

Charan, Ram and Geoffrey Colvin. "Why CEOs Fail: It's rarely for lack of smarts or vision. Most unsuccessful CEOs stumble because of one simple, fatal shortcoming." *Fortune,* June 21, 1999. http://archive.fortune.com/ magazines/fortune/fortune_archive/1999/06/21/261696/index.htm.

Collins, Jim. *How the Mighty Fall: And Why Some Companies Never Give In.* NY: HarperCollins, 2009.

Collins, Jim. *Good to Great: Why Some Companies Make the Leap and Others Don't.* NY: HarperCollins, 2001.

Coutu, Diane and Carol Kauffman. "Coaching: What Can Coaches Do for You?" *Harvard Business Review.* January 2009. https://hbr.org/2009/01/what-can-coaches-do-for-you.

Edleman. "2013 Edelman Trust Barometer Finds a Crisis in Leadership." www.edelman.com. January 9, 2013. http://www.edelman.com/trust-downloads/press-release/.

Gallup, Inc. *Gallup State of the American Manager 2015: Analytics and Advice for Managers.* Washington, D.C.: Gallup, Inc., 2015. http://www.aseonline.org/images/marketing/StateOfAmericanManager_Gallup.pdf.

Gallup, Inc. *State of the American Workplace: Employee Engagement Insights for U.S. Business Leaders.* Washington, D.C.: Gallup, Inc., 2013. http://employeeengagement.com/wp-content/uploads/2013/06/Gallup-2013-State-of-the-American-Workplace-Report.pdf.

Guwande, Amit. "Personal Best: Top Athletes and Singers Have Coaches. Should You?" *The New Yorker,* October 3, 2011. http://www.3quarksdaily.com/3quarksdaily/2011/09/personal-best-top-athletes-and-singers-have-coaches-should-you.html#sthash.h9NYuBGz.dpuf.

Herb, Erika, Keith Leslie, and Colin Price. "Teamwork at the Top." *McKinsey Quarterly*, May 2001. http://www.mckinsey.com/insights/organization/teamwork_at_the_top.

Kaplan, Robert S. and Amy P. Hutton. "Case Study: Romeo Engine Plant." *Harvard Business Review*, November 19, 1993. https://hbr.org/product/romeo-engine-plant/194032-PDF-ENG.

Kaplan, Robert S. and David P. Norton. "The Office of Strategy Management." *Harvard Business Review*, October 2005. https://hbr.org/2005/10/the-office-of-strategy-management.

Lencioni, Patrick. *The Five Temptations of a CEO: A Leadership Fable.* San Francisco: Jossey-Bass, 2008.

Llopis, Glenn. "7 Reasons Employees Don't Trust Their Leaders." *Forbes.com*, December 9, 2013. http://www.forbes.com/sites/ glennllopis/2013/12/09/7-reasons-employees-dont-trust-their-leaders/.

Mankins, Michael, Alan Bird, and James Root. "What 'A' Players Bring to the Table." *Harvard Business Review*, January-February 2013.

McFarland, Keith R. *The Breakthrough Company: How Everyday Companies Become Extraordinary Performers.* NY: Crown Business, 2008.

Michaels, Ed, Helen Handfeld-Jones, and Beth Axelrod. *The War for Talent.* Boston: Harvard Business School Publishing, 2001.

Michelman, Paul. "Working Knowledge for Business Leaders: What an Executive Coach Can Do for You." Harvard Business School, June 13, 2005. http://hbswk.hbs.edu/archive/4853.html.

Premier Executive Forums and Naviga Business Services. *Issues Facing CEOs.* Premier Executive Forums and Naviga Business Services, 2012.

Pritchard, Bob. *Kick-Ass Business and Marketing Secrets: How to Blitz Your Competition.* Hoboken, NJ: Wiley & Sons, 2011.

Ratkiewicz, Katherine and Ted Garnett, "Connecting Organizational Culture to Financial Performance and Business Impact." Human Capital Institute Research & PS Culture Matters Webcast, Tuesday, March 19, 2013. http:// www.hci.org/digest/1629293.

Schmidt, Frank L. and John E. Hunter. "The Validity and Utility of Selection Methods in Personnel Psychology: Practical and Theoretical Implications of 85 Years of Research Findings." *Psychological Bulletin*, September 1998, Vol. 124, No. 2.

Sherpa Coaching. *The Seventh Annual Executive Coaching Survey 2012.* Cincinnati, OH: Sherpa Coaching, 2012.

Index

About the Author

John D. Lankford is passionate about business development, enhancing performance, and achieving results. An expert in executive coaching and developing leadership talent, his fun and lively approach motivates others to embrace their own development, improve their performance, and implement new ideas. To ensure each executive owns his or her development efforts, he emphasizes alignment, individual planning, and accountability to achieve clearly defined goals and dreams.

Lankford has undergraduate and master's degrees in business administration. With more than 25 years' experience developing leaders across a wide array of industries, he has come a long way from his early days as a supervisor on an assembly line at Ford Motor Company's Dearborn Assembly plant, in both production and quality control. Before becoming a Master Certified Business Advisor and a Certified Executive Coach, he was responsible for leadership development at three Fortune 500 companies—Ford Motor Company, Comcast, and Ascension Health. In 2003, Lankford became one of the first 100 consultants to achieve the prestigious Certified Performance Technologist (CPT) designation in Michigan, recognizing those who have a proven track record of improving the performance of organizations.

A significant amount of Lankford's work consists of assisting small, mid-size, and Fortune 500 companies to boost their business performance. His experience in designing a companywide system to develop the next generation of executives has been recognized as "the most comprehensive approach to developing leaders ever seen in corporate America" by the program director at the Center for Creative Leadership.

Before leaving corporate America, Lankford started and eventually sold two of his three businesses. Once he launched his consulting firm, he became a partner in a business coaching franchise. His franchise experience led to an offer to become the CEO of the Innisbrook Leadership Institute in Tampa, Florida, in conjunction with Sheila Johnson. At the round table kick-off event, CEOs were asked to name the top business issue they were facing. Their answers became a white paper that was delivered to the White House days later.

With a dynamic presentation style, Lankford applies his real life experience when a conference keynote speaker. He has been a presenter at the Disney Institute, the Worldwide Conference on Work Teams, and the International Conference for Performance Improvement, to name a few.

Lankford has also served as adjunct business professor at two colleges, and has been an instructor of new executive coaches worldwide. He has designed and implemented executive education and leadership programs with GE, the University of Michigan Business School, and the Center for Creative Leadership. And he has been tapped as an expert business source by prominent media, such as the *New York Times,* CBS, and *DBusiness* magazine, in addition to having been a syndicated business columnist.

Giving back is another of Lankford's passions, and he is proud to have been selected for the Global Award for Abundance and Giving. He received this annual award at a global conference of more than 1,000 executive coaches, and was honored as the person who most demonstrated helping those who needed assistance.

Lankford has been a member of the Lee County Christian Chamber, a board member for Big Brothers Big Sisters, president of the Romeo Chamber of Commerce, an officer for the Lions Club, and chairman of United Way. He was recognized as the 2007, 2008, 2009, and 2010 North American Associate Business Advisor of the Year. And in 2015, he was appointed to the Christian Business Round Table board of directors.